Fire Jewel

Fire Jewel

A Devotional For Freyja

Gefion Vanirdottir

Asphodel Press

Hubbardston, Massachusetts

Asphodel Press
12 Simond Hill Road
Hubbardston, MA 01452

Fire Jewel: A Devotional For Freyja
© 2013 by Gefjon Vanirdottir
ISBN 978-1-938197-09-3

Cover art "Freja i jej koty" by Sylwia "Telari" Cader

Printed in cooperation with
Lulu Enterprises, Inc.
860 Aviation Parkway, Suite 300
Morrisville, NC 27560

To the Vanadis,
who taught me to know my own worth.

Contents

Introduction

The idea for this devotional came from a dream. In the dream, I was sitting in my room, holding this book open in front of me. I could only see that I was reading a poem, but I knew the purpose of the book: that it was a devotional to Freyja, and that I had a hand in making it a reality.

I knew then that this book had to be written.

Ah, Freyja! It's hard not to love her, isn't it? Yet, it is ironic that although she is and was one of the most celebrated goddesses in both the Iron Age and modern times, there is a dearth of devotional material dedicated to Freyja. This collection of writings by many different contributors attempts to remedy that somewhat. Here you will find poems, prayers, rituals, songs, and more in praise of the goddess in her various aspects. To some, she is a goddess of love, others speak of her as sorceress and *seidr*-worker, some see her as the goddess who mourns for her absent husband, others as a mighty warrior, still others as *Mardoll*, shining upon the sea. She is all of these things, and more.

It is my hope that this devotional will inspire and inform, will, perhaps, allow you to see a side of this goddess of many names that you haven't seen before. It is also my hope that this project will inspire other projects of its kind.

This devotional was named for Brisingamen, the wondrous necklace, forged by four dwarves that is the embodiment of her power. In *Þrymskviða,* she becomes so angry at the prospect of being married off to one of the jotnar that the necklace breaks. Freyja is a goddess who knows her own worth, and this is one of the many things she has to teach us.

I've divided this book into three sections. The first section is for articles, the second for rituals, prayers and songs, and other ritualistic material, and the third is for poetry. The people who have contributed to this endeavor come from all walks of life and each has a different take on this multifaceted goddess.

May the words in this book honour the Vanadis.

And may you, dear reader, be inspired by the words within its pages.

GEFION VANIRDOTTIR
AUGUST, 2013

Writing

The Holy Twins
Gudrun of Mimirsbrunnr

Twins were a common sacred theme in ancient Indo-European mythology. They are found throughout the paths of those peoples, from Greece (Artemis and Apollo, Helen and Clytemnestra, Castor and Pollux), from the Celts (the twins of Macha, left over from a number of IE "horse twins"), from India (the Ashvinis), the Lithuanians (the Asvieniai), the Latvians (the Dieva Deli), the Romans (Romulus and Remus), and the proto-Germanic peoples (the Alcis, or twins of the sacred grove).[1] It seems that the concept of two children born at once from a single womb was a sacred event, a sign of abundance and an omen that the Gods had blessed the people.

While there is technically no mention of the Norse Gods Frey and Freyja being twins, it would be contrary to the entirety of the Indo-European culture that bore them into this world if they were not. They function very much as sacred twins in this cosmology, the way that Artemis and Apollo function in the Greek pantheon—and, like them, they are both associated with light-bringing. However, where the Greek twins are celestial, the Norse twins are very earthy and associated with fertility and love. Their names—which are really titles, *Lord* and *Lady*—are somewhat difficult to etymologize, but their seem to be two likely possibilities, much debated. One is that the term comes from the IE word *per*, meaning first or forward, which became the Proto-Germanic *frawan*, or chief.[2] Another possibility is that the word comes from the Proto-Indo-European *Pieheh*, which means "beloved". this word was the root for the names of several love deities and "love concepts", including the Sanskrit *Priya* and *Prajapati*, the Hittite *Purulli*, the Albanian *Perendi*, the Bohemian *Priye*, the Persian *Peri* (elf), and the Greek

---

[1] Ward, Donald. *The Divine Twins*. Folklore Studies No. 19. Berkeley: University of California Press, 1968.

[2] Watkins, Calvert. *The American Heritage Dictionary of Indo-European Roots*. Boston: Houghton-Mifflin, 2000.

Priapos which was Latinized to *Priapus*. At some point, a whole host of P-words were slurred into F-words by the Germanic branch of the IE languages, which is why we have *father* instead of *pater*, *fish* instead of *pisces*, and *Frey/Freyja* instead of *Priapos* or *Priya*.[3]

As children of an Earth Mother and a Sea Father, they are manifestations of food abundance on both land and sea—very important for a culture developed in a place of many coastlines and not much fertile land. Njord's fish were as important as Nerthus's crops, and by creating Divine Twins between them, it was assured that both food sources would function as a bountiful and interdependent whole. The attributes of both fertility and being saviors at sea are part of the repeating characteristics of IE sacred twins.[4] While both twins were probably invoked at various times of the year, Freyja seems to be more associated with springtime while Frey with his Sacrificial Corn King aspect appears later in the year. This would posit them at opposite ends of the harvest process, with Freyja inspiring the seed and flower, and Frey embodying the cutting-down.

Another set of repeating characteristics among twins is association with the Sun—sometimes through a solar/lunar pair, sometimes through twin brothers who are siblings of the Sun Maiden or Dawn Goddess. In the case of the Norse twins there is no lunar theme, but a sort of slurring of the Sun Maiden/Dawn Goddess with a brother ... and again, I emphasize "of a sort". Neither Frey nor Freyja are direct solar embodiments per se, that role being taken by Sunna, but they are both generally conceived of as "golden" deities and are associated with amber and honey, both solar substances. The gold of the Sun and the gold of the grainfields reflect each other, in many historical cultures. The Norse Twins are

---

[3] Mallory, James P.; Adams, Douglas P. *Oxford Introduction to Proto-Indo-European and the Proto-Indo-European World*. London: Oxford University Press, 2006.

[4] Michael Shapiro. "Neglected Evidence of Dioscurism (Divine Twinning) in the Old Slavic Pantheon." *Journal of Indo-European Studies* Vol. 10, 1982.

not the Sun in the sky, but the sunlight that touches the leaves of food plants, which can be conceived of as a separate connection.

In some divine twin mythemes, the twins actually have separate paternities (even though they are born at the same time) which determine their separate fates. This is reflected in the myth of Castor and Pollux, where the divine son of Zeus remains in the heavenly realm while the mortal son dies and must be rescued by his brother. While Njord seems to be firmly the father of both the Vanic twins, Frey dies and is returned to the earth each year, while Freyja does not, echoing the Dioscuri theme. In a sense, one twin ascends while the other descends. On the other hand, Frey is happily married (after a tumultuous courtship) while Freyja is either portrayed as belonging to no one or recently widowed. Her fruitless search for her lost husband may be seen as her own turn at the underworld journey, where Frey rules above with his bride.

One of the most difficult and uncomfortable themes between the Vanic siblings (for modern people, anyway) is the idea that they are sexual with each other. In the Lokasenna, Loki accuses Frey and Freyja of having sex together in public where the other gods could see, and makes scatological references to Freyja's behavior. Njord speaks up for his children and defends their practice as being no shame at all, which may be the echo of an old myth of divine incest coming up against the newer Christian thought, which saw such things as literal and shameful. Western deities frequently marry, fornicate or breed brother to sister—Zeus and Hera, Demeter and Poseidon, Cronos and Rhea, even the Egyptian Isis and Osiris. (While it is not ancient per se, this incest is also echoed in Wagner's *Die Walkure*, where Siegmund and Sieglinde fall in love and breed the hero Siegfried.) In most of these cases (the Egyptian nobility being an anomalous example), it is very much understood by the mortal worshipers that this kind of incest was not for mortals, and would result in disaster if this divine privilege was stolen. Only the Gods could carry off such behavior ... and, really, in creation myths where there are only a handful of children born of a creator deity, who are they to marry except for each other? At any rate, it seems that Frey and Freyja may well have been invoked as a sexual sister-brother pair for purposes of divine fertility.

Another interesting correlation between the Divine Twins is that they are both associated with boars. While modern Heathens tend to concentrate on Freyja's "cat totem", she has a magical boar—Hildesvini—that matches Gullinbursti, her brother's steed. In the saga *Hyndluljóð*, Freyja turns her protégé Ottar into a boar in order to sneak him past Hyndla. Beyond this, on Yule Even the greatest boar was sacrificed to Frey as the sonargoltr, the "atonement boar", to persuade the god to grant a good year, and it is on the head and bristles of this sacred animal that King Heidrek (in *Heidrek's Saga*) and his followers placed their hands and took their most solemn oaths.[5]

The boar is one of the few animals that is reflected in both a wild and a domestic (pig) form; the two are not that far apart genetically, and feral pigs tend to back-breed to boars fairly quickly. The boar/pig is a liminal figure; as a wild creature it is hunted for food and can be tamed to become domestic food, but it always retains its wildness. It is the only domestic food creature that has been known to eat its young. It is associated in many cultures with death goddesses because of this, but not the sort of "deathrealm" goddess that Hel might be. Rather, swine were the provenance of the devouring Earth Mother (Demeter among the Greeks, Cerridwen among the Celts); their colours of white, red and black, their lunar horns, and their fertility (bearing litters of up to ten piglets) show them to be her children. Thus, the pig brings the Twins back to their Mother, Nerthus. One wonders if there is an echo here, with this sacrifice-devouring mother, of the fact that pig flesh has a taste and consistency very like human flesh, due to their omnivorous diet and muscle-to-fat ratio. The pig is the almost-human, between tame and wild, the replacement sacrifice.

---

[5] Chaney, William. *The Cult of Kingship in Anglo-Saxon England.* Manchester, UK: Manchester University Press, 1970.

All research aside, how do I see the Frey/Freyja relationship at the end of the day? As a Freyjaswoman, I know that she has the kind of almost-telepathic deep merging with her brother that many twins have, or are rumored to have. They know when the other is hurting and instinctively reach out, even as they live generally separate lives. I believe that when Frey is in Asgard, away from his wife, Freyja is his solace and gives him special comfort at that time. I also see Frey as being Freyja's anchor in many ways, as she is the more chameleonic of the two. When she is overwhelmed by woe—when she weeps tears of amber—it is often to Frey, the more "settled" twin, that she turns.

They love each other with a love that ranges from childlike and innocent to sexual, yet there is no possessiveness in it. After all, they are both Gods of love, and there is always more than enough love to go around between them. In a way, their relationship is a beautiful example of a loving and sometimes sexual relationship where the participants do not need to be married, or even partnered with each other romantically, for they look elsewhere for those needs. They are not each other's mate, they are each other's other half, which is a different situation. To learn about one is to learn about, and love, the other.

Planting A Freya Garden

Raven Kaldera

As a goddess of love, spring, and fertility, Freya is also a goddess of blossoms, and nothing could be more fitting than to plant her a garden. There are a variety of plants that are associated with her in folklore, as well as some that have become associated with her in modern times, and some that have no particular association, but she would probably love them.

Before we speak of flowers, however, we need to bring in her sacred tree, the Linden (*Tilia europaea*). If you've ever seen a Linden (or Lime, in the UK) tree with its swaying, dancing branches and rustling leaves, it will become clear to you why this is Freya's tree. While Linden trees grow to a pretty fair height and putting one in the middle of a garden might overshadow the plants, the tree could be planted at the edge of the garden and a bench placed under it, for sitting and admiring Freya's garden.

There is a folktale that when Freya first came to Asgard as a hostage, she spent the first year quite unhappy. After the lush flora of Vanaheim, she found the bleak winters and lack of spring flowers to be depressing. When she wept with homesickness, her tears fell to the earth and white flowers sprang forth. In one version of the tale, they are Snowdrops (*Galanthus nivalis*); in another, they are the Lily of the Valley (*Convallaria majalis*). Both these white flowers can therefore be considered sacred to her; they are also small and bloom at different times, and can thus be interplanted. Snowdrops bloom first and will probably be the earliest plant in her garden; Convalilly erupts in May, and was thus sometimes called the Mayflower.

Cowslips (*Primula veris*) were traditionally associated with Freya, as was their domestic cousin Primrose (*Primula vulgaris*). Two old names for the Cowslip flower were "Lady's Keys" and "Password", as they could supposedly be used to travel magically to her hall, Sessrumnir, and get you in the door. They are also golden, as she is. Primroses were originally only pale yellow – "primrose yellow" as it came to be called – but they have been bred in modern times into many different colors. I don't think that Freya has a problem with this, and Primroses of any color can surely be put into her garden.

The wild Daisy (*Bellis perennis*) is sacred to both Freya and Baldur. This isn't the tall ox-eye dairy, but the low-growing tiny one with many petals. Daisy is a warrior's plant, despite its size; it was given to warriors as a good-luck charm, and can be given for the protection of Freya in her warrior form. Its protection extends especially to warriors who are women or nonheterosexuals, as these come under Freya's dominion rather than Odin's.

The harlequin-bonnet Columbine flower (*Aquilegia vulgaris*) is associated with Freya in Swedish folklore, and it became well-known as a supposed aphrodisiac, reflecting her Love Goddess aspect. Potions of Columbine were made to arouse brides on their wedding nights, and during the "language of flowers" era it still meant unbridled lust. In fact, it was considered poor taste to give it to someone you were courting, for that reason. Columbine flowers are actually mildly poisonous when ingested raw, but the immediate poisons break down when heated, so it must be infused in boiling water.

One rather surprising plant associated with Freya is the humble European bean (*Vicia faba*). These, too, can be incorporated into a Freya garden – there are numerous wonderful colors of runner beans, scarlet and white and lavender and pink, with edible flowers. In fact, the center of the garden could be trellises decorated with these annual beans that can twine six feet high or more.

The scarlet Pimpernel (*Anagallis arvensis*) is not one of the plants traditionally associated with Freya, but when I asked, She told me authoritatively that it was Hers. Freya and her brother Frey are both light-bringers and joy-bringers, although the nature of their light and joy is subtly different. The Pimpernel is Freya's joy-plant; its ground-hugging nature and relationship with the sky reflects Freya's earth-goddess Vanic nature that reaches upward to connect with the Aesir sky-nature. It is an antidepressant, and is said to be especially good for youthful girls.

Modern followers of Freya have found that she definitely loves strawberries (*Fragaria vesca*) and the wild strawberry plant, with its intense flavor packed into tiny fruits, is a nice ground cover for the Freya garden. More domesticated strawberry plants can be put in as well. They grow well in pots if there is little room, or perhaps in a "strawberry pyramid" in the center of the garden.

As a last point, while most practitioners will not want to get involved with this plant for legal reasons, Hemp (*Cannabis sativa*) was also sacred to the Vanir Gods and supposedly used in seidhr ceremonies. Beyond this, there are many lovely flowers unknown to the ancestors that are appropriate for this beautiful goddess's garden for their looks alone. Look for golden flowers, for her title as Golden Lady; pink or red ones are for her Love Goddess passion, and white ones are for her warrior side. A few darker purple ones remind us of her role as Mistress of Seidhr. For garden ornaments, amber glass balls recall her favorite stone. Cat figurines symbolize her sacred animal, as do pigs. It's not hard – she'll tell you what she likes.

Life With The Lady

Rhonda Turner

Freya is such a giving and generous Goddess that it is hard to imagine a life without her, for she touches each and every part of my existence. Although I respect, admire and have a limitless amount of love and loyalty for all the Gods and Goddesses of the Vanir and Aesir, it is to Freya that I find myself closest. It is the Lady whom I turn to in times of trouble, and it is she that I first think of to share my joys.

In 1996, when the neighborhood that my husband and I lived in was no longer a safe place to raise our five sons, it was Freya I asked for aid in finding a home in the country. Through her guidance I employed a working comprised of a mother-of-pearl shell one of my younger sons had given me, which I placed in a small container of Holy Water with a small round crystal. By "Holy Water", I mean the water of Urth's Well (time) and the Yggdrasil Tree (space), which can be obtained from fresh running water. Our ancestors' holy sites were often places of power that had both an evergreen as well as running water in the form of a spring or well. They usually collected the water during a waxing Moon, and Ostara was considered an auspicious time to harvest. According to Vilhelm Gronbech, the representation of Well and Tree may well have extended to their altars, since the concept of the *blót* made them indispensable. By using the water of Well and Tree as an aid within rituals or workings, one's intent or need enters the Well, becoming part of the past which then flows forth through the branches of the Tree to become a part of the present. Whispering words, runes, or a charm into a small container of Holy Water is one way of utilizing its innate power. Using this method, the one and only person I contacted about a home returned my call, describing what sounded like a perfect place in a remote hilly area. We agreed to meet the realtor in a small town so that we could try to find the house together.

After driving up and down a dozen maze-like roads of rock and dirt, we finally arrived at the first and only home we were shown in our quest to move from the city. I knew at first sight that it was the place that Freya had found, for I immediately felt like I had come home. The house itself was set upon a hill a far enough distance from the rock road to offer additional privacy, as well as being surrounded on three sides by thick forests of towering trees. As soon as I stepped out of our car I saw—and was amazed at—all of the mother-of-pearl shells that the previous owner had collected. They were scattered around the yard and were also set around a nearby tree, which was also encircled with large fossil rocks. I have no words to describe the love I felt for Freya at that moment—it was totally awe-inspiring!

Entering the house was also a memorable experience, for not only was it larger than our existing one, but it also had a large brick fireplace and numerous windows to better view the surrounding woods. As if all that wasn't wonderful enough, the house was filled with hundreds of hibernating ladybugs. They were grouped in clusters like bouquets along the walls, extending the Lady's warm welcome to our new home. In *Teutonic Mythology*, Jacob Grimm writes that the ladybug was known to be a messenger of Freya. I believe I can well attest to the veracity of this ancient belief. Added to everything else, the home's location offered acres and acres of unpopulated land behind it. The land is a rich tapestry of rolling rocky hills full of thick forests woven with majestic pines, mighty oaks and an abundance of thriving wildlife. There is even a place where a tall evergreen sits upon an overhanging cliff as spring water steadily drips from its partially exposed roots onto a white rock creek bed below.

Needless to say, we wanted to buy the house, but selling our city home would prove to be an almost insurmountable obstacle. Therefore, with Freya's aid I employed a working centered on the original mother-of-pearl shell, and some that I gathered in front of the house. I also created a *taufr* from the bark of an evergreen growing on the property, which I named and blessed with Holy Water. Each month I reddened it with menstrual blood and recited a charm to honor its essence. Over the next five months I felt deep despair at times, for I truly couldn't imagine living anywhere else. Every weekend we would drive the hour and a half trip to just walk the land and be where we as a family now felt was our home. The turning point for me was simply letting go. Although I desperately wanted to live there, the important fact was that I would have the love of our Gods and Goddesses no matter where we lived. Sometimes it seems that the releasing of a necessity is imperative so that it may then come true. Soon after, we signed the papers on March 21st of 1997 and moved in over a two-day period.

I have experienced other wonderful events since then, but the magic of Freya and her ladybugs will always warm my heart. It has also totally convinced me not only of the existence of our Gods and Goddesses, but as well the reality of their ability to manifest their will upon our earthly plane. In truth, it was Freya's guidance that created the workings toward the goal of moving to a home in the country. It wasn't I who found this beautiful place, nor did I ever imagine the house inhabited by her tiny messengers. A couple of days after moving in, the ladybugs took flight in our new home and were everywhere. There were so many, in fact, that it was almost impossible not to collide with them while walking—it was as if they were expressing their joy at our arrival.

Maid/Mother

I think one of the reasons that Freya is considered a Great Goddess is that that she contains both masculine and feminine traits, although her emphasis is more towards the Maid or dynamic half. As Mother she displays the characteristics associated with the Elements of Ice, Water, Earth, and the Moon, which are usually perceived as magnetic energy. These qualities are often associated with the feminine and are apparent in her by-names of Horn (Flax), Mardoll (Sea Bright), and Gefn (Giver). Freya is also called Vanadis, indicating that she is the leading Mother of the Vanir ancestral line.

As a Maid she has many of the characteristics associated with Wind, Fire, and the Sun which are often described as masculine or dynamic energy. This is quite apparent in her role as a Battle

Goddess; Syr (Sow) is often considered her solar aspect as a Warrior Goddess. Another Maid-like aspect is the she-goat Heithrun, for it definitely underscores aggressiveness and intense sexuality. Perhaps an underlying aspect of Maid/Mother is that of two halves equaling a whole, which then yields a third concept of the Wise-Woman. A Wise-Woman could be described as one who has learned to balance the energy, enthusiasm, and passion of the Maid with the patience, perseverance, and wisdom of the Mother.

This concept of Maid/Mother can be seen in the story of Gullveig and Heidh in the First War between the Aesir and Vanir. Of the thrice reborn Gullveig we are told in the *Voluspa*—"ever and anon: even now she liveth." One might surmise from this stanza that Gullveig then must still exist within Heidh. If this is true, then Heidh is not only the Mother aspect, but is also Heidh/Gullveig or Wise-Woman. Heidh is successful because she retains the dynamic attributes of the Maid, while tempering them with the attributes of the Mother. This interplay of dark/light, night/day, moon/sun, ice/fire, feminine/masculine, and magnetic/dynamic is a common theme throughout Germanic myth and lore. It extends from the myth of creation of the Worlds and the Gods from the elements of Ice/Fire, and can also be found in many of our deities' personalities or attributes.

It seems that the dynamic qualities of Air, Fire, and Sun are most often found in the Warrior Gods or Sons, such as Baldr, Fro Ing, and Thorr. This is also true of the Maids, such as the Valkyries who are associated with Wind and Fire, or Mengloth the Sun-Bride and her Nine Healing Maids. It also seems like the Father or Elder Gods are more often associated with magnetic energy, such as the Moon with Mannus, or Njorth with Water, and Odin the "Hidden God" which might align him more with Ice, North, or Night. One then might assume that the Mother Goddesses such as Frigga, Nerthus, and Frau Holda who have Water, Earth or Ice as dominant attributes might also then be associated with the Moon, even though the Moon is considered masculine. This seems a possibility since the Sons or Warrior Gods are often connected to the Sun, which is considered feminine in the ancient Germanic culture.

The interaction of Maid/Mother can also be found in the ancient Field or Corn Ceremonies, as well as many of the customs involved with the event of a birth. *Roles of the Northern Goddess* by H.R. Davidson (pages 68-78 and 124-153) is a treasure trove containing many references and examples of these rituals. Frazer's book *The Golden Bough* contains an interesting chapter—"The Corn-Mother and the Corn-Maiden in Northern Europe." The practice of a "corn dolly" within these customs was fairly common. The last sheaf was dressed as either the Corn Maid or Mother, who often traveled in a wagon and was given a place of honor, as well as partaking in the dancing and festivities at the Harvest Feast. In some areas both were represented with the concept of Maid/Mother working together or one taking over from the other during the year, and at Harvest a baby of straw was sometimes added.

Part of the role of women at Harvest time included aggressive behavior toward men, usually in the form of pranks such as drenching or threats. Another aspect of Harvest was a strong element of sexuality, which included lewd humor and behavior. These customs of aggressive behavior and strong sexuality can also be discerned within their Birth Rituals. The prevailing custom in Denmark during the 19th century was for several women to move into and virtually take over the expectant Mother's home, while only allowing the husband entrance if he came bearing gifts. After the birth a wild drinking celebration often ensued, and as the women traveled homeward they often played pranks on any man they met along the way. They were known to divest men of their trousers or fill their hats with excrement, and engaged in wild and wanton dancing. Harvest and Birth are both events usually associated with the role of the Mother, yet our female ancestors also deemed the Maid's role important, which can be discerned by the inclusion of pranks, threats, and overt sexuality.

Freya's Nine Names

Hail to Freya! Lady of Dark and Light,
Our Lovely Lady of Day and of Night.
Maid/Mother of Seith-craft both Black and White,
Hail to the Mistress of Magic and Might!
Gullveig—Thrice-burnt Thrice-born—Fair Maid Greedy for Gold,
Through All-Time and All-Tides—Seith's Van-Bride shall be Bold.
Heidh—Seith-Mother known as the Comely and Clever,
Wise-Ones will welcome Heidh—Anon and Forever.
Hreda—Our Beauty of Bliss gives Birth to the Spring,
As Queen-Maiden and Mate—of Noatun's Carnal King.
Mardoll—Guardian Goddess of the Shining Seas,
She Wards Well our Safety—and Grants Comfort and Ease.
Mengloth—Healing Mount's Lovely Mistress and Sun-Bride,
Nine Maids of Well-being—Bide Steadfast by Her side.
Horn—Flax and Fate the Spae-Mother Flawlessly Spins,
Always the All-Knowing—Our Trust and Troth She Wins.
Syr—Our Sorceress and Sig-Maiden of the Sun,
As a Skillful Sword-Bride—Her Just-Battles are Won.
Gefn—The Divine Dis-Giver's Tender Touch shall Heal,
Our Mystical Mother—Bestows Health, Wealth, and Weal.
Heithrun—Wild and Wanton She Mates with Earth's Kin-Folk,
A Shapely Moonlit Maid—Veiled by Night's Velvet Cloak.
Praise to the Ladies of Dark and Light!
Praise to the Ladies of Day and Night!
Praise to Freya—our Mistress of Might!
Praise Her Nine Names and Their Blessings Bright!

Symbols and Sexuality

Maid and Mother seemed to be of one mind on the subject of sexuality. While the Maid's main focus is more on the passion and the pleasure the sexual act brings, the Mother's emphasis is perhaps more on the fertility of the fields and the continued production of life in general. Freya has a close association with the element of

Earth, easily discerned since Earth's center and core is sexuality, which she displays profusely and with pride. The myriad of flowers we enjoy throughout the year are a testament of this; the prettiest part—the bloom—are the flowers' sexual organs proudly displayed for all to see. If we observe Earth's children—the wildlife, birds, and even the insects—they are all shameless sexual beings. One of Freya's symbols is the heart, which defines her lusty nature, as it depicts the female form bent over as an outline of buttocks and genitalia.

Another of Freya's symbols is the wain or wagon. The fifth rune of the Elder Futhark is Raidho (Riding), often defined as a wheel under a solar wagon. As a solar rune, it rules the natural cycles of the seasons, the division of night and day, as well as humanity. It expresses the concept of right ordering that therefore results in right action. Raidho is a rune that is an aid in all forms of rhythmic skills, such as poetry, dance, music, and math. Although it is mostly associated with Thor and his chariot, Freya and her wain have a strong correlation with this rune as well. Cats are another symbol assigned to the Lady, both domestic and the wild variety, for her wagon is drawn by large cats. It is easy to see why since the cat is a creature of innate beauty and grace, as well as its fearless, sensual and sexual nature that so mirrors the essence of Freya.

The Sun-Wheel, a circle containing an equal armed cross, expresses the Sun's might interacting harmoniously with the four cardinal directions or elements. It is a sacred symbol that is very expressive of the Brisingamen's ("Fire-Necklace") energy. I often use this symbol as a salute when approaching the altar. One can trace its outline with *gand*, *sax*, fossil or holey stone, or with a closed fist (the rune Raidho). One can also envision being in the center of the equal-armed cross which to me represents the element of Earth. The North point of the cross would then be Ice, East=Wind, South=Fire, and West=Water. An offering to Freya can be made by what I call Dance of the Dwarves or Dancing the Directions within the equal armed cross. It is a ritual to reenact the sacred event of her accomplishment of obtaining the Brisingamen by having intercourse with Northri, Austri, Suthri, and Vestri. It is the main tool that she utilizes as a force of fertility, which can be perceived as one that encompasses all that passes within the workings or the cyclic changes of nature, human rites of passage, as well as willed manifestations within the Nine Worlds. It only stands to reason that since its creation was forged by an agreement of sexual union, its core essence is comprised of a strong energy of sexuality. Therefore, it is a dance that is deeply sensual and sexual in nature.

Seith-Craft

The mythic model of Freya acquiring her magical tool the Brisingamen, to me anyway, is not only a primal pattern for aligning oneself with the Lady, but as well is an expression of the sacredness of sex. The concept of sex as sacred is quite perceivable among the Vanir, as can be discerned in the written works we have. Our myths and sagas make it clear that Freya shared her sexuality with many (divine, dwarves, humans). One message we can take from this is that one's face need not be beautiful/handsome, nor must one's body be perfectly formed. Tall, short, fat, thin matters not, for within each of us is a sexual being. Perhaps then it is our sexuality as well as our individuality that are the attractive aspects of each of us. Seen through our Goddess Freya's eyes, sex is a sacred and joyous source of energy exchange that as well expresses the celebration of life.

The gifts or offerings that I have found that Freya appreciates are many. Incense or candles, poetry or flowers, even the food left for wildlife, but her favorite is enjoying my sexuality. As long as the sexual act harms none or is desired by the sexual participants, all can be offered as a gift. When dedicating your sexuality as an offering, it often heightens and intensifies one's overall sexual feelings as well as the orgasmic outcome. Within my own experience of sharing my sexuality, some of the results have been the building of strong bonds, bridging the gap between human and divine, and forming ties of unbreakable trust.

Another method of sharing sexuality, of course, is the Dance of the Dwarves that I mentioned earlier. The dancer will need music with a steady rhythm to "ride" that inspires the sensual within them. Sitting while rocking back and forth or side to side can be employed instead of dance since the basic idea is the same. It may also allow for a fuller focusing on the bodily senses, therefore permitting feelings of sexuality a wider range. Other possible aids are incense, a candle upon the altar, holding a small piece of amber and/or crystal, and a welcoming toast. Although the latter is not a requirement, the use of alcohol within ritual is an ancient custom that was used by our ancestors.

The dance can be enacted in several ways, but the main goal is to welcome each Dwarf and their Element with the desire and the sexuality of one's most sensual self, thereby inviting their presence in a sexual way. Forming bonds of trust to engender goodwill is the main goal, so it is not about barring or keeping out. Instead, it is an offering of warm welcome and an incantation of invitation. Dance or rock "riding" the rhythm, exuding sexuality as does the essence of Earth and our Goddess Freya, thereby drawing with one's desire, openness, and magnetic ability the energy of each Element. This type of dance may often lead to light to moderate trance, which I've come to think of as a Fire-Trance, since "riding" a rhythm is an intrinsic aspect of attaining this state. When I first started this ritual, it was to mirror and honor Freya in a re-enactment of her own dance of desire in obtaining the Brisingamen.

In her book *Leaves of Yggdrasil*, pages 186-187, Freya Aswynn mentions knowing of two different trance types. One, which comes naturally to her, she describes as an almost somnolent state in which the mind is turned inward, which I think of as the Ice-Trance. The other type she defines as exhilarating, leading to a tremendous amount of energy, and (in my experience) may also include such an extreme state of ecstasy that I have often shed tears of joy. This type of trance has various levels of altered consciousness. One of the most memorable was being entirely encircled in a bright light flecked with gold and silver sparks that emitted wave upon wave of total unconditional love. It was an all-encompassing, all-consuming state of bliss and ecstasy.

During this type of Fire-trance state I received my initiation into the runes of the Elder Futhark. I had been studying the runes intensively for several months by reading all the books on the subject that I could find. (Edred Thorsson and Kvedulf Gundarsson were among the sources I found most helpful.) The need for learning was almost an obsession, and every spare moment was devoted to obtaining and absorbing any and all facts known about the runes. This may sound like a chore, but I felt driven and found each new piece of information exciting. My mind was near exhaustion when one night I experienced the runes during a moderate trance state, merging with them through orgasm and ecstasy. Each rune appeared before me blazing a bright fiery red while filling me with bliss and joy. Although I have not read of this occurrence before, I ascribe it to Freya since her nature is so sexual. Freya and Odin are known to have shared with each other their respective crafts, so perhaps when Freya shares her rune knowledge it may well be received in this manner.

The next morning when I awoke, I still felt fairly ecstatic, as I often do after a Seith trance. The amazing part, however, was that all the written words that I saw were runes. Wherever I looked, be it a book, billboard, or television, I couldn't see the ordinary letters visible to others; instead I perceived them as runes. This was not a short or momentary event either, for it lasted over a period of several hours. My favorite part was during our ride to see the country home we were trying to purchase. Large billboards dotted the landscape along the way and all proclaimed their wares with giant runes, it was truly an awe-inspiring experience. Soon after this incident, I collected and started crafting the wood for my own rune staves. The process was lengthy, for it took nearly a year to inscribe and redden with menstrual blood each of the twenty-four staves three times, but it has been well worth the effort and time I invested. Receiving the runes during a Seith dance-trance by no means made me a rune master, but it certainly helped clarify and bring together the knowledge that I had gathered.

This type of dance can as well be offered to honor other Gods and Goddesses. Odin, Fro Ing, Thor, and Njorth are examples of masculine Gods who appreciate this energy, while Nerthus, Idhunn, Freya, and Frigga work well as examples of Goddess energy. Combining masculine and feminine energy such as with Odin/Frigga, Sif/Thor, or perhaps Nerthus/Njord, Fro Ing/Freya, is another option. Even one's fetch-animal can be called to in this manner.

After the ritual is over, I've found it helpful to ground any excess energy. This can be accomplished by placing hands on the floor and sending it to Mother Earth, or sending it into a crystal or ritual tool to later be used within a working. Although at times I have performed a working within the Fire-Trance, more often it is used for the exchange of passion, pleasure, and sexual energy. Most of my workings for prosperity, protection, healing, etc. are done at another time, by calling upon the bonds already formed with the essence of the divine: ancestral, elemental, or other of Earth's kin such as trees. At these times I may use items such as Holy Water, body fluids, herbs, candles, and stones, but the toasting is usually omitted.

Working tools that can be found easily within one's body include blood, menstrual blood, saliva, semen, and vaginal fluid. Hair and nails seem to be acceptable items and are employed for healing or hexing, weal or woe, the energy directed by the one who uses them. The other blessings of our body are often not discussed, for they are still regarded for the most part as too primal, repugnant and even "evil". However, these gifts or tools that reside within us are certainly as effective as external ones (if not more so) for endowing our workings with our energy and our will. If we distance ourselves from these "evil" sacred sources of the body, we then may run the risk of losing part of the tools of our heritage. Heathens who work with blood in relation to reddening runes know that there is a definite energy in this substance that links them to ancient past ways. Women who are of child-bearing age have the extra advantage of a monthly supply without the need to cut their skin to reach the source. I found it a tremendous tool just within the scope of trance work, for one can use it to write runes or sacred symbols on the body. For example, I have ritually inscribed the Algiz rune upon my face several times. It gave me a very warrior-like or Valkyrie-like appearance, and the ensuing (moderate) trances were absolutely awesome and beautiful. Our ancestors were wise and knew that blood held power as well as promise. When I use blood in rituals or workings, I know that I rekindle and revive a flame that has dimmed at times, but will never be extinguished.

Body fluids such as saliva, semen, and vaginal secretions are also mediums of power. Saliva is mentioned within Anglo-Saxon charms of magic, usually as spitting to avert ill-will by returning it. It was also used as a form of healing by expelling illness, thus spitting to bar its re-entry. The mingling of saliva, as seen within the myth of the Aesir and Vanir's creation of *Kvasir* after the First War, is also a substance that can be employed to build bonds. By and large sexual fluids are often viewed at best as a messy nuisance, but to me they are extremely useful and joyful sources of energy. Semen and vaginal fluid are excellent substances to use within all areas of workings from healing to hexing, but are especially good for those of growth or gain. Within my own experience, I have found vaginal fluid itself to be nearly as powerful a substance as one's monthly flow. I often work with the energy of Fire contained within candles used for workings; when doing so, I anoint their surface with Holy Water and with this wondrous fluid that issues forth from the dark well-like area within my woman's body. To my mind, Christianity at least retained some of the concepts of our ancestors—the body is indeed a temple and a sacred sanctuary. However, they have endeavored over the centuries to erase other common-sense Heathen concepts, in that the body fluids contained within the temple are also sacred, and a blessing to be utilized.

I have mentioned dedicating one's sexual act with words, as well as honoring Freya and the dwarves through dance or "riding" which can lead to a light or moderate trance state. Another ritual of importance is performed for the purpose of sharing one's earthly body and sensations with a God or Goddess. It is thought by many that for the essence of the divine to manifest upon our mundane plane, a vessel or container is often required, which was probably the reason our ancestors looked to birds and other beings for omens to guide them. This being so, an offering that is appreciated is the temporary sharing of one's earthly form with the divine. The ritual is similar to Dance of the Dwarves, but is different in that in addition to a sexual union of orgasm, it is also an opening or sharing of one's body. In my experience it is an occurrence of true sharing, in that you are aware and part of the entire process. We often take for granted the many pleasures that are housed within the bodies that are ours; hearing, seeing, smelling, tasting, touching and even movement can feel truly exquisite. When sharing these experiences of the senses, one's own pleasure is enhanced and increased. Also, the wonder and "newness" of the unnoticed, those things perceived so much as a part of one's everyday world, is a unique feeling which is hard to express. As way of exchange, riding on the back of Battle Boar across the darkened skies lit only by starlight and the glowing bristles is one of my favorite events to see through Freya's eyes within her world.

The method I often use is similar in many ways to Dancing the Directions. Movement or "riding" is an aid in opening one's being for entrance of the essence of another as well as the offering of a toast or two. The main difference is intent, which can be expressed with words of invitation. Sexuality is, of course, a part of the process, for all of our Goddesses are sensual in their own individual ways. All of those who I have worked with seem to love to feel the movement of arms and legs in motion, and when dancing one may feel such a surge of energy flowing that it almost seems as if one's body is flying. When sharing my body, I am always amazed at how effortlessly it moves, with an almost orchestrated precision. Freya's essence seems often to prefer a faster steady beat to "ride", while Frigga and others may at times desire a more moderate type of music with beautiful melodies.

If privacy allows, utilizing an outdoor setting is good, for it is our most primal source of rhythms to "ride". Standing on Mother Earth and opening your being, you can sometimes actually feel her essence, almost like the drumming of her heart. Wind as it brushes and caresses your skin adds its own rhythm, as does a flickering fire or the lapping sound of waves within a lake or ocean. As one becomes fairly adept at being open, occasionally you may find that ordinary movement may bring on short stretches of sharing one's body without any other aid. This has happened to me several times, most often while walking in the woods. The best way I can explain the experience is that it is as if a veil is removed from all of your senses. Everything that you normally see becomes indescribably beautiful and seen with total clarity. This applies also to sounds and smells which are awesome in their heightened intensity; for me it is always a welcomed occurrence. Freya has touched and transformed my mind, heart, body, and soul. Her love has given me the ability to open my being, enabling me to know that she and I have danced before, and will throughout all time.

Brising's Earth-Bride

Hail to our Carnal-Queen–of the Dance-Trance Embrace,
Wise Women Shall Seek Her—Through All-Time and All-Space.
As Brising's Earth-Bride, Ever shall Freya Abide,
Within the Sun-Wheel's Center, as Mentor and Guide.
The Maid/Mother of Wild and Wanton Abandon,
All Adult Acts of Sex, She deems Sacred and Blest.
A Sensual Sorceress, Nipples Pertly Proud,
Taunt Belly and Buttocks Do Tease and Tantalize.
Ever Pounding, Pulsating, Throbbing and Thrusting,
As Lithely She Leads the Erotic Rhythmic Ride.

The Undulating Union of Sheath and of Sword,
As well the Mystic Mating of Ring and of Rod.
Entwined in the Threads of Time of Gold/Silver Light,
Ever Dance We the Dance of Desire and Delight.
By Body, Breath and Soul, Ferth and Fetch, Hugh and Heart,
Freya Shall Stay Within—Our Each and Every Part!

Tree Above The Cave
Rhonda Turner

View From The Cave
Rhonda Turner

Tools of Seith-Craft

Rhonda Turner

Freya's art of Seith-Craft includes the use of many types of tools. The Sun, Moon, and Elements of Ice, Wind, Fire, Water and Earth are of course a core part. Much of Freya's wisdom was destroyed by the onset of Christianity, for they found her primal passion and shameless sexuality distasteful, and therefore often referred to her in derogatory terms. Fortunately, one can never totally erase an imprint that is as strong and true as the essence of our Lady, for she is encoded within our very being.

The part of Freya's craft of Seith that I am most familiar with is the utilization of the sexual energy of one's body, which then merges with the sexual energy that is inherent in the essence of the divine, as well as all that is of nature. A good example of what I am referring to are our Earthly Kin of trees. They are mighty sources of energy, wisdom, and lore, as our ancestors well knew. Their roots delve downward into the dark depths of Mother Earth, yet at the same time their branches arch upward, touched by Wind, Water, Moon, Sun, and Sky. They are therefore supreme synthesizers of dark and light, for within them opposites become one.

Behind our home is a magnificent sixty foot evergreen, encircled with fossils and holey stones, which I consider my personal representative of the World-Tree in our myths. To me it is a doorway to divinity, for as my arms and thighs grip the rough bark of its large trunk, I have ridden roads to other realities. Uniting one's sexual energy with a tree through orgasm may not be the method the Druids used, but it does work. Perhaps it is even this type of joining that inspired, in part, the image of the witch riding a besom. Sexual union with another being brings one as close as possible to being one, while retaining the separate essence of each. This exchange of energy also builds a bond of trust, for it is not one-sided; this regal tree has returned all that I have given. The bark upon its base is freely given, and I have found no finer wood to inscribe runes upon or use for other workings. To me it is not only a mighty Tree-Steed, but a link and column upon which messages can be sent and received.

Altars/Harrows

The altar is assembled by your creation, a place that you assign and set aside as a bridge between worlds. It is a sacred area that you craft to honor the essence of the divine, ancestors, nature, concepts, and myths; as such it expresses the center and core of one's self. In most books written about our Germanic religion the altar is usually referred to as a harrow or *horgr,* in olden days this often meant a pile of stones. Today an altar is referred to as a harrow no matter what material is used to create it, although an inside altar may also be called a stall. Altars are personal and can range from the austere and uncluttered to almost every single space of area being occupied by something meaningful. One can also have a single altar or several; having many in no way will lessen their worth. I mention this because I have had the time and the means to create quite a few harrows. Living in a heavily wooded and fairly isolated place has been advantageous for this purpose. The items within the altars I've created are merely suggestions to build upon rather than being an absolute necessity in your own altar creations.

Indoor Altars

I have several inside altars, such as the one for Frigga that is centered on the wood dining room table in front of a large picture window. It seemed an appropriate place for the Goddess of Hearth and Home, since from this prominent place she can survey most of our living area. Beside her I have created smaller images of her handmaidens Hlin and Fulla, to emphasize Frigga's important roles of protection and prosperity within the household. Sometimes I light a candle and set it in front of her image when asking for aid or expressing gratitude.

If you have a fireplace, the mantel above may also serve in a general sense as a harrow; if not, perhaps a wooden shelf could be used. My husband made our mantel out of a long piece of Fir. I carved runes upon its front to express love and loyalty to our Gods/esses, as well as other sacred symbols. Several purchased images of our deities and a created image of our Idises find themselves upon the mantel, occupying a central place of honor within our home. On each side of the hearth, pillar candles are set and lit nightly with words of gratitude. Each Yule-tide I buy a grapevine wreath which I cover with evergreen boughs I have harvested, and hang it above our fireplace. Then, at Twelfth Night (New Year's Eve), we hold the wreath, each pledging our loyalty and the year's promises, and then watch it burn within the fire. Other wreaths to celebrate the Blessing-tides throughout the year are also hung over the mantle.

The main harrow within my home is located in the bedroom, which I would imagine is not uncommon since it is an area that offers privacy. This is a plus for sex rituals, and overall allows for less distraction, which is an advantage for focusing intent within all workings. The top of a wood dresser or table is good, and if one can arrange for it to set against a North or East wall, then all the better.

Items gathered from nature (or a basic form embellished with feathers, stones, shells, etc.), can be crafted as representations of our Gods/esses. Freya's is formed from a basic straw shape to which I added a "falcon-feather coat" (a soft rabbit skin with feathers attached) and her "Brisingamen necklace" (small wooden beads painted and hung on red thread). Nerthus is made from a piece of wood that I found that contains a naturally embedded stone that juts out like breasts. I attached a holey stone shaped like a head to the top of the twig with red thread and placed the figure within a small wooden wagon. For both, I braided cotton cords of red, white, and black to attach around their waists. I found a twig shape that consists of arms, legs, and a part that looks much like an erect penis for Fro Ing; adding an acorn head gave him quite a dapper look. A small skull with horns found by one of my sons seemed appropriate for Njorth. To add my own touch, I inscribed his name on the horn and skull area in red runes. There are many possibilities for creating forms to symbolize our Gods/esses; the only limiting factor is imagination.

Other items on or beside the altar include a container of Holy Water, a votive holder for candles, an incense holder, wands of wood or stone, a wooden blessing bowl containing two natural stones (one male/one female in appearance), a red leather pouch with runes, various fossils and holey stones, *taufr* in progress, a sax (knife) that had belonged to my Father, and a representation of Thor's Holy Hammer, as well as other items from nature that I find on walks. (From this description you may be able to surmise that the altar I've described would not be classified as austere or uncluttered.)

One other core element that seems central in importance to me is a representation of Earth, Well, and Tree. The myth within the *Volsupa* of Urth's Well and the evergreen Yggdrasil is one that, from the beginning, has resounded deep within my being. Before moving here, my husband, sons and I would drive nearly two hours to reach a lake area where I could collect water from a natural spring. Quoting from *The Well and the Tree,* Paul Bauschatz writes: "The spring is one of the clearest natural representations of the bounded, welling water source. If the well is the well of the past, into it would be gathered all actions; likewise, it would supply strength and guidance." I am very fortunate to presently have an awe-inspiring place to collect Holy Water. About a half a mile behind our home, I walk until I reach the bottom of a fairly deep ravine. Far above at the edge of an overhanging cliff, a tall evergreen sits, spring water steadily dripping from its partially exposed roots onto the white creek bed below where I collect the water.

Harvesting the water of Well and Tree struck such a resonating chord of truth within me, that I longed for its representation within my area of sacred space. I expressed this initial intrinsic need by placing a white holey stone on the center front part of the altar, and within the stone's opening I placed a small evergreen branch. Although the stone and branch still sit in center prominence, soon after we moved here I felt a further need to define the visual effect even more clearly. I started with a small well-like container that I filled with earth and small white rocks. Next I placed an evergreen twig within the white rocks. The small branch I chose basically resembles an Algiz rune in shape, and to enhance the primal image, it has a phallic pine cone still attached to the twig. To reinforce the representation, I placed an eagle-shaped stone at the top and a dragon-shaped one upon the white rocks.

As mentioned before, I always have a container of Holy Water upon the altar for workings and rituals. It is also present because of the esteem in which I hold it as being the Water which links All-Worlds and All-Past/Present times. At times I pour this water over the symbolic Tree, whispering words while it slowly flows into the Well of white rocks/Earth. Bauschatz writes, "*Gylfaginning* 16 adds the act of watering the world tree Yggdrasil to keep it 'evergreen'. The Norns nurse and sustain it; as such, their activities have a positive and generative force. The holy water, through which the nurture is accomplished, comes from Urth's Well." He further states, "Just as the water of the well brings its power to the world tree, just so the past actively brings its force to bear upon the affairs of the world. All present existence is contingent upon the continual control and support of an active, nutritive past." My thoughts are that by imitating the actions of the Norns, one acknowledges and perhaps adds in small part to the dynamic interaction of Earth, Well, and Tree. It is also a way to not only respect and hold in high regard our ancestor's worldview, but to embrace and make it my own as well.

The first indication I had that the ritual described above might have occurred in ancient days was while reading *The Culture of the Teutons* by Vilhelm Gronbech. In Volume 2, under the sub-heading *Symbolism of the Sacrificial Place,* Gronbech writes:

> The altar contained a symbol representing the useful, fruitful earth, probably consisting of a heap of mould. The ritual of this cosmic mould is *aurr*—"earth is called aurr among the high gods," we learn from the didactic *Alvismal.* The aurr is styled white, certainly not on

account of its colour, but in allusion to its purity and its holiness, its power of cleansing and blessing. This sacred symbol is further called the power or luck—megin—of earth (e.g. Hynd. 39), and from such formulae as that mentioned in Gud. II 21, we learn that it was used for purposes of consecration, mixed up with other sacrificial ingredients such as water and fluid from the kettles ... The sacred tree and the well belonged to the holy places outside, but the principle of the blot rendered it indispensable that they should be represented on the altar. When it is said that the rivers take their rise in the centre of the world, it is identical to saying that they flow from the feast and spring from the ideal—i.e. the real—world situated on the altar in the sacrificial place ... In all probability the tree was carried into the hall in the form of a branch or twig. The cosmos of the Vsp. being, as we have seen, drawn against the background of the feast it becomes probable that the volva, who says she remembers the time when the tree was beneath the mould, has before the eye of her mind a dramatic situation previous to the moment when the branch was planted in or at the side of the aurr.

Later in 1999 I read *Freyja: The Great Goddess of the North* by Britt-Marie Nasstrom. She states that in stanza 19 of the *Voluspa*, the tree and well were combined with white "aurr", which she says means "gravel" and further writes that it has been interpreted as gravel mixed with water. In Hollander's *The Poetic Edda* the Old Norse word *hvitaaurr* is translated as meaning white dew, and in Larrington's version it is translated as "shining loam." Nasstrom as well offers Gro Steinland's theory of the word hinting at a cultic ritual where *hvitaaurr* is poured over the tree. "The pouring of *hvitaaurr* describes a cyclic process and suggests an affinity between well and tree."

I think from these passages that we can conclude that our ancestors held Urth's Well and Ygg's tree in high esteem, so much so that not only were they an important aspect of their blots but of their harrows as well.

Outdoor Altars

Having lived in a fairly large city for an extended period of time, I can empathize with the difficulty of creating an outside sacred space. Even a privacy fence doesn't really offer privacy, plus one's neighborhood is often filled with the distractions of a variety of noises. Having a small mobile wood harrow and enacting rituals late at night is one option; driving to a more secluded spot is another possible method for overcoming this lack of privacy.

Our main gathering area for blessing-tides or blots is located in a secluded place not far from our home. My husband and sons constructed a sturdy wood harrow and six small bench seats crafted from the same wood, with the same design. The benches are arranged around a fire pit that is encircled with fossils, holey stones and bricks on which I have painted runes and sun-wheels. Trees play an important part, for North of the harrow stands an ancient and awesome tree dedicated to Freya's father Njorth, with many holes that act as compartments for offerings. To the West is another tree that it expresses much of the might of Frey, for it has a very long phallic-like protrusion. The phallic-like trunk angles out from the base of a full grown tree. To honor Frey's sexual essence I placed a round decorated wreath upon the phallic shaft as an expression of male/female union.

I found a wonderful tree within the woods to dedicate to Freya's mother Nerthus. It is a tall tree with a large trunk that near the ground is rounded as if swollen with life and ready to give birth. Under the swollen area is a hollowed out opening perfect for leaving offerings. The tree for the Idises has three trunks coming up out of the ground, leaving a bowl-like area in its center. It is circled with fossil and holey stones, as are the trees I've dedicated to Frigga and other of our gods and goddesses.

Herbs

I heartily recommend *Medicine of the Earth* by Susanne Fischer-Rizzi, a resident of Salzburg, Germany. Not only is this book beautifully written, but as well contains excellent offerings of illustrations and information about Germanic folklore. In this book, the author introduces us to "Blessing the Herbs", a custom long celebrated by Heathens to request the blessing of the Goddess to be bestowed upon the gathered herbs. This ancient custom was usually enacted between August 15th to September 8th, when herbs were harvested in bundles of seven or nine. Mullein held the place of honor as the center of the herbal grouping. Other probable herbs are St. John's Wort, Arnica, Centaury, Wormwood, Valerian, and Yarrow, to name but a few. Once harvested and tied into bundles, the herbs were offered to the Goddess to bless, and then placed in their homes or thrown into the fireplace to ward against lightning, as well as hung above barn doors. It was a tradition that was perceived as a way of offering gratitude to the plant's essence as well, since it provided both magical and medicinal properties to one's family throughout the year.

Angelica

This is a plant well known to our ancestors for it is found through legends and myth in Iceland, Greenland, and Norway, and was prized for its healing abilities. Containing the energy of the Sun, Angelica was known by the old German name of "Fearwort". Nordic skalds wore wreaths of the flowers as a crown to inspire themselves with joy and confidence. A protective herb, it can incense, in healing rituals, added to bathwater, or sprinkled around the home.

Arnica

This herb is associated with and named after the wolf; some of the German folk names alluding to this are "Wolf's Eye" and "Wolf's Yellow". Other names include "Wellbestow", "Thunderwort", "Strengthwort", and "Woundherb". These names express the high esteem in which our ancestors held this herb, for they indicate not only healing qualities, but its magical might as well. Arnica, along with St. John's Wort, Male Fern, Mugwort, and Calendula, are all known to have been utilized in Midsummer rituals. It is used in healing salves to treat sprains and muscle soreness, but it is not to be taken internally, and may cause dermatitis.

Arnica.

Calendula

Also known by the common names of Pot Marigold and Garden Marigold. The plant's German folk names are "Rampant Flower" and "Curl Flower". Calendula is one of the flowers that belong to a group called "Bride of the Sun", as is the Daisy, Chamomile, Dandelion, and Chicory. Each turn and travel with the Sun's progression, their flowers following it throughout the day. Since it blooms from June to late summer, this plant and Chicory are considered traditional flowers for the Autumnal Equinox or Holy Harvest on September 23rd, which is a good time to honor the Vanir. Calendula is representative of undying love and believed to be a plant capable of producing magical love, since it provides and puts forth new blossoms all season long; therefore it is known as the "Never Wilt Flower". According to old lore, if the herb is harvested at noon, it will have the ability to comfort, gladden, and strengthen the heart.

Priestesses referred to as "Sun Brides" were well known as seers and for their healing abilities. Fischer-Rizzi writes that they lived in the hills of Germany, in an area named "Women's Mountain" (*Frauenberg)*, and further states that the Sun Brides were dedicated to Goddesses such as Freya. This lore is very similar to the story of Mengloth and her Nine Healing Maids that can be found in *The Lay of Svipdag (Svipdagsmal)*. In this lay Mengloth is referred to as "the sunbright maiden" and "goddess of gold" that Svipdag arduously seeks so that she may become his bride. Mengloth and her nine maidens live upon Lyfja Mount, meaning "Mountain of Healing", similar to the Women's Mountain of the flower folklore.

Cowslip

Hildegard von Bingen was an Abbess during the 12th century and her writings are recorded in *Physica,* which preserves much of the Heathen beliefs still known about the various herbs of northern Europe. She wrote that Cowslip was known by the name of "Heaven's Keys", and deemed it as gaining all of its energy from the Sun. This herb has always been associated with the feminine

Cowslips

forces of Venus and the Sun. Freya was the Cowslip's earliest northern patron, and much of its lore is specifically about our Vanic Goddess. According to folklore, the Goddess was known to carry a small golden key (a symbol of the Cowslip) tucked away within her crown. This tiny magical tool was associated with Freya's ability to unlock both the human heart and the power of Earth, thereby waking the slumbering elements of nature for the forthcoming fertility of the growing season. The Cowslip is considered an important and integral part of Ostara rituals, since it is a time that celebrates the dawn of day and the Sun's cycle of regaining in strength. This is shown by the burning wheels our ancestors rolled down slopes to imitate the Sun's passage through the dark and dying winter into the rebirth of light within spring. At this solar tide, round loaves of bread symbolizing the Sun were blessed and eaten. The Heathen roots of Ostara's current custom of coloring eggs and hiding and hunting them began long ago in Germany.

Ground Ivy

This plant in particular was a primary meal ingredient during a celebration known as Green Thursday (or Maudy) that occurred before Ostara. The custom was to gather nine green herbs and then to make them into what was called "Green Thursday Soup" or the "Soup of Nine Herbs". These nine herbs were often dedicated to the Goddess, especially in her aspect as the life-giving Mother, and eaten  outside. Other herbs that may have been included are Stinging Nettle, Ribwort Plantain, Daisy, Chickweed, Dandelion, Yarrow, Speedwell, and Ramsons. Our ancestors perceived this partaking of the green plants of nature as a way of aligning themselves with the divine, the elements and energy of nature, and the spirits of home and hearth. Celebrants danced throughout the night while wearing wreaths of these herbs, to symbolize their link with the divine and the energy of nature.

Some of Ground Ivy's folk names are associated with its wreath usage, such as "Earth Wreath" and "Wreath Herb", and it was used as well at Walburga's Day for this purpose. Ground Ivy's name in German is *"Gunderman"*, which translates as "Pus Man," since the plant was and still is seen as a kindly elf-man who warded and gave strength to those inflicted with wounds which might become infected.

Hemp Agrimony

Common folk names for this plant are "Deer Clover," "Deer Wound Herb," and "Deer Heal". These names refer to the fact that hunters had observed wounded deer seeking out and consuming this herb. In modern day it is used for washing wounds and is taken internally to hinder infection, since it is known to increase the white blood cell count. Being a plant so strongly associated with deer, an animal sacred to  Freya's brother Frey, it has long been considered to be dedicated to him. It is an excellent herb in workings of protection, for it not only shields but returns ill-will to the sender. Hemp Agrimony or Boneset's other powers as a plant seem to center around its magical ability to affect the weather. These weather workings were often enacted on March the 3rd. Known by the folk names of "Thunderherb", "Weathershrub", or "Cold Weatherwort", burning Hemp Agrimony was a popular weather-spell to employ.

Lady's Mantle

 The folk name of "Heaven's Water" for this plant refer to its leaves which curl or cup, thereby collecting dew or moisture. Some old German folk names are "Dew Cup" and "Fair with Tears", as well as the O.H.G. *Sintau* meaning "Ever-Dew." For our ancestors, Freya was the Goddess known as the patron of this plant, especially since its main medicinal usage was as a woman's remedy. It was gathered during the waning Moon to halt the blood flow of women and was also used to treat wounds. Modern medicine concurs with our ancient ancestor's knowledge, for it is used today to help harmonize the female system in several ways. Magically, it was employed in love spells and sachets.

Male Fern

Male fern has long been known for its magical powers. Fern fronds were perceived as symbolizing the spiral, known to represent good luck and healing. Spiral dances around the fire were often enacted to align with the divine, nature, and the energy of the Sun. Ferns were usually gathered at the solstices and hung in homes and barns for protection from illness, and women placed them by their bed to promote fertility. The root was carved into a small hand shape and worn as an amulet to strengthen and ward off illness.

Mugwort

This herb was once known as the "Mother of all Plants", and was perceived as a gift from the Goddess. It was also associated with Thor and his great girdle of strength, *Megingjardr*. Some of the old German folk names of Mugwort are "Thorwort", "Power Wort", "Girdle Wort", and Solstice Girdle. Our ancestors braided Mugwort to be worn at Midsummer rituals, since this day has long been considered that of the Sun's peak of power. Those wearing the braided herb did so to honor Thor and to align them with his strength for gaining good health and endurance throughout the year. At the ritual's ending, the Mugwort girdles were either thrown into the fire or kept for their warding power and hung in homes or barns. An amulet of its root was made and worn to gain its strength and healing ability. Magically, this herb has many uses, such as cleansing and charging crystals, wearing to increase strength or for protection, increasing lust, and easing depression, to name a few.

Mullein

As previously mentioned, this plant was considered the central herb in the bundles harvested for the custom of "Blessing of the Herbs". An old German folk name for Mullein is "Demon Plant" since it was thought to ward against spells and disease. Our ancestors believed Mullein to be a kindly magical being that could aid and protect them. It was also known by the name of "Weathercandles", for it was thought to have the ability to avert lightning from striking. Even today in some rural areas it is grown beside homes for this purpose, but never brought inside for fear that lightning might follow it.

Primrose

The Primrose, like the Cowslip, has long been a flower dedicated to Freya. This correlation is easy to understand, since it popularly represented wantonness and sexual abandon. It is said that blue and red Primroses grown around the home are not only protective but as well attract the Fair Folk. It is useful in sexual rituals and can be carried in herb bags to dispel depression and attract love.

650. Primula vulgaris Huds.
Primrose; Y.

St. John's Wort

During Midsummer rituals this plant is prized and placed upon altars. It was—and still is—worn as a head wreath while dancing around a bonfire to renew one's connection with the divine and the energy of the Sun. Fischer-Rizzi describes St. John's Wort as, "golden five-petalled blooms radiating like small sun-wheels around a shower of bobbing stamens". It has long been known that the plant is at its peak when gathered on

Midsummer Day, and even more so if it is harvested with early morning dew upon it. Our ancestors perceived the dew as the sacred water left from the wedded bliss of Heaven and Earth, and an Icelandic custom was to roll in it to become strong and healthy. Wreaths of St. John's Wort were often thrown upon roofs as a protection from lightning; a bit could be sprinkled upon the hearth for the same purpose.

Valerian

This plant is also commonly called Garden Heliotrope, and it is the root that is harvested in October for herbal use. The English deemed this herb as "All Heal" for its ability to treat various ailments, but its best known attribute is as an effective sedative. The German folk name is *"Baldrian"* after our Germanic God Balder, son of Odin and Frigga. Magically, the powdered root is utilized in protective sachets, as well as in pillows to promote sleep. Its calming effect could also be used in love sachets and to ease arguments. Valerian is also called *"Velandsurt"* or "Wayland's Wort", perhaps in connection to the sleep draught that Volund gave to Bothvild in *The Lay of Volund*.

Stones

The stones mentioned here are but a small selection of those that are available, but they are the ones that I have worked with the most often. Metals, as well as stones, are usually classified as either projective (Fire) or receptive/magnetic (Ice). Gold and Fire are closely connected as having sun-like properties that are conducive to prosperity, healing, courage, and confidence. Silver and Water are often linked to the magnetic abilities of the moonlight and are used within workings to increase one's subconscious awareness for divination, psychic activities, healing, and dreams. Copper is a metal associated with feminine energy and can be an aide in balancing or harmonizing the body as well as stimulating healing.

The shape of the stone is an aspect often considered as an indicator of the ability inherent within it. A round shape is usually indicative of heightening magnetic attributes, and as such can be utilized for attracting prosperity or healing, or absorbing an illness. Those that are long and phallic in shape are prized for their projective powers, and can be used in a wand-like manner for sending and for other workings. Square shapes are usually deemed to contain earth-like energy, and are useful in promoting stability, for healing, and in prosperity workings. Diamond-shaped (or Ing-shaped) stones promote prosperity and attract riches, while heart-shaped ones attract love and can increase lust.

There are different methods one can use to cleanse and charge stones. Crystals, and others with Ice attributes, I usually put in a small container of Holy Water and place in the moonlight. Amber and those with Fire characteristics do well in Holy Water when placed in sunlight. Another method I've used is placing the stone within a well-like container of earth or salt for several days, which is especially good if you've purchased the stone and want to totally cleanse it. Before using a stone within a working, I often sprinkle it with Holy Water to reawaken its inherent ability, thereby increasing its effectiveness and enhancing the outcome.

Amber

Amber is the fossilized resin from prehistoric pine or coniferous trees. Some pieces contain fragments or complete beings that were once alive, such as insects or plants. Strongly associated with the Sun, it is often described in terms such as being a piece of solidified light. Its other energy is expressed by the evergreen qualities from whose sap it is comprised, which define the eternal. It is associated with Freya and Thor and their fiery attributes, for when amber is rubbed against certain materials it projects an electrical charge that draws small pieces of paper or other light objects to cling or adhere to its surface. Although it has projective power, it also contains this magnetic essence that is expressive of the sensuality so much a part of Freya's nature. Amber's uses are many and varied, it is considered to be one of the oldest stones for healing. It can increase and strengthen rituals or workings when placed upon the altar or held in the hand. It is an excellent source to utilize during sexual rituals, as it increases one's strength and sexual enjoyment.

Bloodstone

A stone often termed the "Stone of Athletes", since it is believed to increase strength, courage, confidence, and endurance. A deep green stone with flecks of red, considered a stone of healing which may aid in decreasing the flow of blood. It also has a reputation for increasing prosperity and is thought to aid in legal matters or court cases.

Flint

Associated with Fire, shaping, and craftsmanship, Flint is also known by the names of "Thunderstone", "Elf-Arrow", and "Elf-Shot". Long valued for its powers of protection and healing, it was often hung over windows and doorways

Fossils

A favorite pastime of mine is walking through the woods while searching for fossil stones, and I almost always return with the most wonderful treasures. I have some stones that are almost entirely comprised of intricate fossil shapes. Some have worm-like shapes imbedded in the stone, while others are like small wheels with many spokes radiating out from a center axis; I have even found entire seashells turned into stone. Although fossils are often deemed to be receptive in power, I have some phallic-shaped ones that I utilize as wands within rituals and workings. Due to their ancient age, fossils are often worn as amulets, or placed upon the altar as an aid to increase one's energy and an overall aid with the ritual or working.

Holey Stones

A Holey Stone is any type of stone that has a naturally occurring hole within it, usually the result of erosion caused by water. Our ancestors also called Holey Stones names such as "Woden's Stone" or "Odhin's Stone". This is in reference to the All-Father changing into the shape of a serpent in order to bore a hole-like entrance through the side of a mountain, in order to recover *Kvasir,* the stolen mead of poetry. It was created as a truce to end the war between the Aesir and Vanir so that bonds of troth would exist; thus *Kvasir* contained the energy and essence of both, and was of the utmost importance.

Stones that contain within them other naturally occurring stones are prized as being powerful amulets of protection. They are also hung upon red thread or cord above doorways, windows, and structures containing animals. Holey stones are used for healing purposes by placing or rubbing the affected area to absorb the ailment. As with fossils, phallic-shaped ones can be utilized as wands. Another useful method is to whisper runes or say an incantation through the stone's opening.

Jet

A black stone that is formed from fossilized wood that is millions of years old; like Amber, it becomes electrically charged when rubbed. It is considered a stone of good luck and protection, and wards off nightmares. Used in healing, it works by absorbing illness or negativity, thereby granting harmony and balance within the body. Jet is also useful in workings of divination as it increases one's awareness.

Lapis Lazuli

Other than the Holey Stone, Lapis is the one most often mentioned in relationship with Odin, as well as the Ansuz rune. It is said to be a mental and spiritual opener, aiding one in receiving both the message of the hidden mind and the inspiration of the gods. Lapis is highly valued for its overall essence, which promotes the powers of one's mental, emotional, physical, psychic, and spiritual abilities. A beautiful blue stone, it is also deemed to bring joy, opening one's ability to give and receive love. Healing and bringing harmony to mind and body are also within its scope of abilities.

Lodestone

A few other names for this stone are "Magnet Stone", "Way Stone", and "Hercules Stone". Thor is representative of this stone's potential and power; it is known to strengthen workings by drawing energy to them, and aids a successful outcome. It is also exceptional in its ability to draw disease or pain from the body, as well as being considered an aid for impotence. It should be cleansed and charged between uses, and some recommend Linseed oil as an aid.

Mother-of-Pearl

Mother-of-Pearl is the iridescent or multi-colored portion of shells found at many lakeside areas. I can certainly attest to its abilities, especially if paired with the power of a round crystal. They are an excellent enhancement for a working to draw a desired outcome. The effectiveness is also increased by placing both within Holy Water, or even by adding a pinch of salt. I think of Mother-of-Pearl as the Wish and Weal Mother, for she is a wonderful aid within prosperity workings and for the purpose of protection.

Quartz Crystal

Probably one of the best known stones, and by far the one most written about and utilized for magical purposes. Perhaps more than any other, it is receptive and projective, programmable in its energy to activate, transmit, send, store, and focus. One can utilize this duality of direction by employing a small round crystal as well as a terminated crystal (the six-pointed is my favorite) in each hand or beside one's working. It is an aid in all types of endeavors, whether it's healing, harmony, or divination, and of course in all workings to increase psychic awareness. Quartz Crystals come in different natural colors, such as Rose Quartz for love or harmony and Smokey Quartz for grounding and decreasing depression. All are excellent for their varied purposes, but it is the clear kind that is the king/queen of their field of expertise.

Blessing-Bowl and Blessing-Twig

The wood blessing bowl I use sits upon the altar in our bedroom, holding male/female stones when not in use during Blessing-tides or blots. The blessing twig is usually a small evergreen branch that is harvested with words and an offering right before the ritual begins. Although our ancestors used the blood from the sacrificial animal that was to eaten during the blot, Heathens of today often use water, mead, ale, or beer. Whatever fluid is to be used to bless those gathered, it is placed within the well-like structure, and the evergreen twig is then used to dip into the bowl to collect the fluid, which is then sprinkled on those assembled at the gathering.

Gand or Wand

A wand is a very useful tool. It can be comprised of a variety of substances including stone, wood, herb roots, or bone. The one I use most often is phallic in shape and was created by my husband. It is made from a female Osage Orange tree, and although this is not a traditional wood in the Germanic sense, many of the tree's attributes seem well suited to the fiery aspects of Seith. The tree has glossy lance-shaped leaves, stout thorns, tightly woven branches, an orange cast to its bark, orange roots that yield a yellow dye, and small green flowers in May or June. The female tree produces a 3-5-inch bumpy fruit called a hedge apple, which ripens in September or October. The milky juice inside the fruit acts as an insect repellent, and the only edible part is the 200 interior seeds which squirrels are known to love. A hard, tough, durable tree, it transplants well, regenerates from stump sprouts, tolerates poor soil, extreme heat and high winds, and has very high BTUs when burned. It also has the distinction of being a warrior's wood, since it is considered by many archers to be the world's finest wood for bows.

Being a phallic wand given to me by husband, I decided to dedicate it to Frey. Overall it is eleven inches; the upper shaft is very smooth, while the lower half is still encased with bark, giving the wood wand a definite energy of phallic power. I inscribed runes and sun-wheels on the smooth part, the bark shaft, the tip and end. It is perhaps one of my most magical tools, for it can be used as part of a sex ritual, and the sexual energy harnessed within can be utilized later for a working. It also can be employed within Fire-Trance rituals, as it can be held and ridden between the legs. No matter what type of wood is chosen, I highly recommend a phallic wood wand.

As a wand dedicated to Freya's brother, a ritual to honor virile *Volsi* may be enacted. In the writings of *Flateyjarbok,* we read about a family where the horse had died, and the wife had saved and preserved the stallion's very large phallus. Every evening she said spells and lewd verses over it, ending with the refrain, "May Mornir receive this sacrifice." "Mornir" (troll women) is known as a kenning for Skadhi and Gerd, and is also a recorded name for a sword. *Volsi,* the horse phallus, is the emblem and embodiment of Frey, the God of Fertility.

Sax or Knife

The main sax that I have is used for inscribing sacred symbols or runes on the surface of bark, wood, and candles. I have also employed it as a sending tool, or even occasionally as an "opener" to facilitate a door-like result. A single-blade sax is usually recommended, and it can be as ornate or simple as one chooses. As mentioned, the one I have once belonged to my father and is special since it represents his lineage and essence within my work. Most magical tools within modern Heathen practice are given their own name and then sprinkled with water, as in the ritual of blessing a nine-day-old child.

Whip or Scourge

The scourge is not a tool often mentioned, for it seems to be perceived as the proverbial "black sheep". The one my husband made for me has nine black leather strands, eighteen inches long with a small knot at each end, attached to a small bark-covered branch. It has significant value in erotic rituals, and for those who enjoy the sexual act of pain/pleasure, it can be dedicated as an offering to the divine. I have used the whip lightly across my back and buttocks during ritual dance several times. In addition to the steady beat of music, it offers another rhythm to "ride" that can be an occasional dance/trance tool.

The other main purpose for the scourge is during the Yule-tide celebration that honors Frigga, Frau Holda and the Disir at Mother-Night. The basic ritual can be found on pages 268-270 in Kvedulf Gundarsson's book *Teutonic Religion.* When we have the celebration, it is somewhat shortened, and I added Freya and Nerthus to be included in the list of Mothers. In this ritual, the mother gives each family member a light tap, saying: "That for the year's woe—may it wane in the year to come." Then she offers each a small gift, saying: "That for year's weal—may it wax in the year to come." It is a ritual that my sons really enjoyed, and if you have children you might consider making it a part of your own Mother-Night tradition.

Jewelry

A representation of Thor's Hammer is an effective way of warding oneself at all times. It also expresses one's Heathen troth and ties to our Eldest Kin (Gods and Goddesses) and Elder Kin (Alfar and Disir). As mentioned before, small holey stones can be worn as amulets and runes, or sacred symbols can be scratched or painted upon their surface. Another article of jewelry that I always wear on the same chain as the Hammer is a pillbox locket. It can be any type of locket that allows small meaningful objects from nature to be carried near your body at all times. In doing so, it is a tool that enables a continuous connection to nature, and an expression of love and loyalty to Freya.

Hammer

A representation of Thor's Hammer hangs on the wall to the right of our main indoor harrow. It is crafted to be an emblem to honor Thor and to emulate the might of his Holy Hammer Mjollnir; therefore it is an important tool for warding sacred space. Suggestions of a wooden sledgehammer or a hammer with an oaken handle are those most often mentioned within modern Heathen books. Other written sources convey the concept that the original form of Mjollnir was an axe made of stone, in part because of rock carvings dating from the Bronze Age. Stone axe-heads were conceived of as the very embodiment of thunderbolts throughout all Germanic countries.

Whether you choose a representation that is a hammer or an axe, the important factor is that it feels right to you. I searched for some time before I found one at a flea market that was right for me. I knew as soon as I touched its old oaken handle that it was the one. It is axe-like in appearance, having blades upon both sides, and the smaller blade resembles the Thurs rune in shape. On the oak handle I inscribed the name *Mjollnir* in runes, and also inscribed two Fylfots on the axe head and two on the hammer's handle. To charge it with Thor's blessing and energy, it was taken outdoors during a thunderstorm. I also use methods of blessing the Hammer with Holy Water, a kiss, or with vaginal fluid.

I have experienced several memorable incidents concerning the weather, but perhaps the most amazing involved our Lord of Lightning. It was a summer's day in 1999, the skies were filled with heavy gray clouds and the echoes of distant thunder resounded in the distance, warning all of his chariot's forthcoming approach. I had wanted a way to express more fully my love and loyalty to our Guardian God, so I decided that I would dance for him. Thor's Hammer in hand as my only attire, I walked to our main outdoor harrow. As I walked the wind started to blow in earnest, while the clouds churned and were very low to the ground. When I arrived at the firepit lined with stones, I faced South, the direction from which the storm was approaching. With both hands gripping the handle, I raised the Hammer aloft in greeting. Before I could utter a word, the lightning lit up the sky, right where the head of the axe was pointed, the sound of thunder encircled me, and a hard drenching rain issued forth. The wind wildly whipped my long hair, and the lightning, thunder, and clouds were so close I felt that I could have reached out and touched them. Instead, I sang my love and loyalty in chant and runes, and as I sang I danced around the fire pit to honor the Protector of Midgarth and Men. I'm sure I should have been frightened, but instead I felt an indescribable sense of exhilaration and energy, for it truly was a beautiful and awe-inspiring experience.

Although some might not think of Thor's Hammer as a tool of Seith-craft, I have included it within dance/trance rituals. It can be held aloft and used to inscribe symbols in the air or held between the thighs and "ridden" while dancing.

Omens

In closing, I thought to include the topic of omens, since they were certainly a tool utilized by our ancestors. The cries and the flight of birds were observed for signs that carried messages from the divine. Swallows, eagles, and storks were thought to bode well, while the owl, dove, and cuckoo were believed to be beings that brought bad tidings. Ravens, boar, cattle, and horses were not worshipped for themselves but because they represented and embodied the essence of a God or Goddess. For their will or desire to be known upon our earthly plane, our Gods and Goddesses require a vessel to house their energy. These birds and animals were messengers between worlds. Sacred horses, for example, were regarded as the mouthpiece of the gods among the Germans, and signs were divined from their neighing and snorting.

Although these are quite valid methods, I am more of the mind of discerning any signs that are out of the ordinary. If you live in a city and being outdoors isn't within your schedule, omens may not occur as often, but are not impossible. I mentioned before the many ladybugs that took flight soon after we moved into our home in the country—to me that was an omen of Freya's pleasure at our arrival, her way of rejoicing with me at finally attaining the home held so close to my heart. The ladybugs still come visit our home at times, covering the outside walls as well as sharing their company with us inside. Candles are another indoor method of receiving an omen. After particularly intense Fire-trances I have seen the flame of a candle become much brighter as well as rise quite high—to me a sign of confirmation at how well the ritual had went.

If you have access to privacy within an outdoor setting, then your chances to receive an omen are more likely to occur. They are not an everyday happening, but that makes them all the more treasured as occasions. Once when I was sitting outside while squirrel hunting, an eagle soared right overhead, looking directly into my eyes. Another time as I was walking down to harvest Holy Water I saw a spider peeking down at me over the rim of the hat I had on. When I took it off, I could see it was very large and colorful. Once I might have counted as a coincidence, but on the walk I encountered two more large spiders, just as colorfully attired.

There have been other omens I could share, but I will end with one that I've never shared with anyone other than my husband. I have it recorded in my journal as happening on May 22, 1998. I was going down to the evergreen tree that I mentioned at the beginning of this article, singing runes as I walked, when two does stopped not far from where I was and seemed to be listening intently. I stopped walking but continued singing; this went on for ten minutes before they slowly moved on. When I arrived at the evergreen I sat down on the bench, which is set a few feet from the tree. Overhead a crow flew by so I called to it by singing runes. Before long 12-15 crows flew overhead and started to fly in circles above me. As they continued to circle above, two more came and landed near the top of the tree and looked directly down at me. Tears welled up and trickled down my cheeks as I watched the two within the tree and the others encircling me overhead. After they all left, I felt somewhat shaken, but thrilled by such an otherworldly and totally awesome omen. As if to assure me that the event had actually happened, a few minutes later they briefly returned, flying in circles above me once again, then in unison they all flew to the West.

Previously, I would never have thought of telling anyone since it is an extremely mystical omen, which happened on an ordinary walk in the woods. I am older now, perhaps a little wiser, and find myself wanting to share with others the greatness of our Gods and Goddesses. Freya is my guide, my mentor, the one I turn to with my joys and sorrows. As we dance throughout the strand of time together, she will always be my center and core.

Eldest, Elder, and Earthly Kin

Walking within the Woods—Embraced by the Wind's Soft Sigh,
'Tis an Encounter of Enclosure—of Earth and Sky.
I am Warmly Welcomed—by this Place of Awe-Power,
Through All the Sacred Seasons—at Each and Every Hour.
One's EI-Self Awakens—Within the Woods Ur-Altar,
Past/Present Meld and Merge—Sure Footsteps Shall Not Falter.
Eldest Kin and Elder Kin—Ay Walk these Woods with Me,
On Raven's Wings, Spider Webs—or a Towering Tree.
Omens of Air and Earth—Gebo's Link for Gods and Men,
Bright Beings of Z-Exchange—Ever our Earthly Kin.
To Earth and Sky, North, South, West, East—Ice, Fire, Wave, Wind,
Praise-Poems I Fain Shall Offer—Ygg's Runes I Shall Send.
I Hold the Horn on High—to Honor the Holy Host,
Eldest, Elder, and Earthly Kin—Hear this Heathen's Boast.
I Pledge and Promise—Love and Loyalty from my Heart,
Throughout All-Days and in All-Ways—Never Shall We Part!
By Fire and Ice, by Water and Wind, by Well and Tree,
By Earth and Sky, by Moon and Sun, So It Ay Shall Be!

Glossary

- ଔ Ay—Used in the *Poetic Edda* to mean always.
- ଔ EI—The EI-rune, Eihwaz, 13th rune of the Elder Futhark, which in part contains the concept of the eternal evergreen, life within the winter of death.
- ଔ Fain—Gladly, also used within the *Poetic Edda*.
- ଔ Gebo—(Gift) 7th rune of the Elder Futhark, contains the mystery of two being one.
- ଔ Hugh—Also *hugr*, *hige*, or *hyge*—meaning intellect or mind.
- ଔ Perthro—Container used to throw lots. The 14th rune of the Elder Futhark, which is deemed a symbol for *orlog*, it is as well the rune of time and therefore linked to the Norns. Part of Perthro's essence is that of "constant change—that always remains the same".
- ଔ Thewful—Used in the *Poetic Edda* as meaning strong, mighty.
- ଔ Ur—A prefix used to indicate primal.
- ଔ Wih—Holy, set apart from the mundane.
- ଔ Wit—To know.
- ଔ X—The shape of the Gebo rune.
- ଔ Z—Used to indicate the 15th rune of the Elder Futhark, Elhaz or Algiz, which as part of its essence expresses the connection between gods and men.

Freya by Halo Quin

Ritual

Invocation to Freya

From the Pagan Book of Hours

Hail to Freya the Vanadis!
Lady of the Vanir whose soul
Is bound to the Earth, the seeds that grow
And yet stretches forth into the mists!
In the winter we hail you as Lady of Love,
Warming our cold nights with your smile.
In the spring we hail you as Earth-Awakener,
Breaking open the seed that sprouts.
In the summer we hail you as Gatherer of Warriors,
Taking those to your breast who catch your eye.
In the autumn we now hail you as Lady of Seidh,
Wise sorceress who speaks with spirits.
Open the veil of vision for us, wise Vanadis,
And may our sight penetrate down the line of blood to the future.

Four Directions Freya Ritual

Gudrun of Mimirsbrunnr

This ritual was created for a Pagan gathering, to educate a group of people who knew nothing about Norse work about the Goddess Freya, and her different aspects. Everyone sat in a circle, and I had laid the altar to the Vanadis in the center. Laid around it were four handmade cloaks which I had created as ritual vestments for her workings. There were also four wreaths, and four other items that went with each of them. (I wore only a simple white shift, which would go with any of the cloaks.)

In the North lay a cloak that was a patchwork of spring green and different fabrics printed with spring flowers. Its lining was a brilliant green satin. The wreath was silk flowers in spring colors, with many dangling ribbons. Next to it lay a basket of flower seeds.

In the East lay a cloak of gold – the color of honey, of amber – with jewels sewn onto it, and a lining of a rich rose color. The wreath glittered with gold and amber-colored beads, and there was a basket of strawberries (which were fortunately more or less in season at that point; if they are not, you might want to try some other fruit).

In the South lay a cloak of snowy white with a hood of artificial brown "hawk feathers", cascading down the back like wings, and a scarlet lining. The wreath was also of brown feathers. Next to it lay a sword.

In the West lay a cloak of dusky purple, embroidered all over with bind runes and magical sigils. The wreath next to it was of odd-looking curly weeds covered in glitter, and there lay my staff, which is actually like a carved cane. (Burial finds have shown that the seidkona's "staff" is actually what we would today consider a cane.)

I begin by lighting a stick of dried mugwort and carrying it all around the circle, blessing each person with it. Then I begin in the North. I put on the cloak and wreath in the North and pick up the basket of seeds, saying:

Let me tell you about Freya, the Goddess of the Vanir. The Vanir are a tribe of Gods whose job is agriculture – the creation of food. They aren't the only food-producing Gods, but they are the experts! Freya is the Daughter Goddess among them, the daughter of Earth Mother Nerthus and Ship-Father Njord, and the sister of Frey the God of grain. Even though she has two small daughters herself, every Spring she comes up as the Maiden, bringing the cold Earth to life. This is Freya's first face.

I walk around the circle, scattering the seeds. Then I walk around a second time, giving a few seeds to each person present, saying:

As she walks on the new Spring earth, the sleeping seeds in the ground awake, and new green springs up in her footsteps. All the Vanir are Gods of fertility, and Freya is no different. As the Spring Maiden, she is the Queen of the flowers, the blossoms that blaze from each stem of green. Take these seeds with you, and plant them, and when she arises and blossoms, praise her name! Hail to you, Earthly Maiden! May you bless us with the blossoming of new beginnings.

I go to the North part of the altar and carefully lay out the flowered cloak and wreath, and lay down the basket. Then I go to the East part and don the golden cloak and wreath, and pick up the basket of strawberries, saying:

The second face of Freya is as the Goddess of Love. She is no virgin, but the one who opens her arms to many – men, women, young and old, beautiful and ugly. She chooses, yes, but she chooses not by our standards but by hers, and her standards are unknowable. She is beauty – glowing, living, sparkling beauty, with the brightness of the Summer Solstice. She is the suddenness of love that you did not expect, blowing you off your feet like the wild Spring wind, filling you with new possibilities. Taste her sweetness!

I walk around the circle, giving fruit to each person present, saying:

Once four dwarven brothers, great smiths and craftsmen, made the most beautiful necklace in the world, a thing of spun gold and amber and jewels. Freya saw it, and asked for it herself. The dwarves asked a price of her favors for four nights, one night for each of them. Freya agreed, because she knew that her great beauty and skill at love was a fair price for their great skill, and for the most beautiful necklace in the world. She knew that she was worth that, and it was no insult in either direction. And though the other Gods looked askance at her, to this day Brisingamen, the most beautiful necklace in the world, lies around the neck of Freya. Hail, golden Lady! May we learn to open our hearts to others – and more importantly, may we know our own worth when we do it!

I go to the East part of the altar and carefully lay out the golden cloak and wreath, and lay down the basket. Then I go to the South part and don the falcon cloak and wreath, and pick up the sword, saying:

The third face of Freya is as the Warrior. Long ago when Freya came to Asgard as a hostage after the war between the Gods of Earth and Sky, she made a bargain with Odin who chooses the slain warriors to take with him. Freya bargained to be allowed to choose one-third of the slain, and to be the first to choose – and she won! She especially loves woman warriors, and particularly handsome men. She flies over the battlefield in her cloak of falcon feathers, which give her the form of a fleet falcon, spying on the bloodiness below, among the watching Valkyries.

I walk around the circle with the sword, pointing it at people whom Freya might take, if they died in battle, saying:

As a Love Goddess who also knows how to wield a sword, she shows us that Love is not passive and helpless. Love is strong and passionate. Love knows how to fight to protect dear ones. Love knows how to make hard choices. Love knows how to fight to protect one's own boundaries, that the garden may stay healthy and not be overrun with weeds. Love is when you have each other's back. Hail to the Warrior who sees the best, and knows to take it! May you bless us with the courage to love ourselves as well as others.

I go to the South part of the altar and carefully lay out the falcon cloak and wreath, and lay down the sword. Then I go to the West part and don the sigil cloak and herb wreath, and pick up the staff, saying:

The fourth face of Freya is that of the mistress of Seidr, the magical arts. She is the mysterious sorceress who can tell the future in the smoke, who can make a charm of love or vengeance, who can call the fish to the bay and the deer to the hunter's arrow-tip. She is the music in the spell's incantation, the circle dance around the fire with the wishes flung forth. She is the patron of hedge-witches, fortunetellers, and farm-wives who charm their cows into better milking. Would you know your future? Touch the staff of the seidkona, and perhaps a word will flash into your mind. If it does, speak it aloud or be silent, as you will.

I walk around the circle holding out my staff, so that each person can touch it, saying:

This is your gift from Freya – a tiny window onto the future. Hail to the Lady of Magic, you who are the love-spell and the love-song, who can look into the future and speak it to all those gathered. Hail, Lady, who draws back the dark veil and lets the golden light shine through! Be with us in all four of your brilliant faces! Hail the Vanadis!

All shout, "Hail the Vanadis!" and the rite is ended.

Agricultural Charms For Freya

Geordie Ingerson

For a Lime Tree

The Lime tree, or Linden tree, is Freya's tree, with its graceful fluttering leaves. Anyone who has seen a Lime tree dancing in the wind will agree. The leaves are brewed into a tea to reduce nervous tension. If you have a Lime tree, hang colourful ribbons on it to honour Freya, and bless it with this prayer:

> Vanadis, Golden Lady,
> Dancer on the spring earth,
> Maiden who brings joy to the heart,
> I consecrate this Lime with love,
> Its leaves shall laugh and sing your praises,
> And you ever shall be honoured here.

Blessing the Flower Garden

Flowers are all Freya's (except for ones that are specific to certain gods or goddesses, and even then they will probably admit that Freya is friends with their special plant too). The flower garden plays an important role in the life of anyone who must create their own religious rituals alone or with a few friends. Monasteries of old had flower gardens so that they could have altar decorations throughout as much of the year as possible, and this is still important for the lone Vanic practitioner.

> Lady of spring snowdrops,
> Lady of summer cowslips,
> Bless my acre of beauty
> With your perfect golden touch,
> Bless the offerings to come
> That all might enjoy, and you as well.

To Protect the Henhouse

One tale I've heard, which may be a rumour but if so it is a lovely one, is that the Pleiades were once seen as Freya's hens. To guard a henhouse, paint seven spots on it like the Pleiades, and then say:

> Vanadis, my feathered ones keep
> Safe from stoat and marten's teeth,
> Safe from fox and feral dog,
> Bedded safe in nests to sleep.

For a House Cat

What would a home be without the housecat curled up by the hearth, or on a comfortable lap? Beyond this, cats are a good way to get rid of the mice that are a constant problem in country houses. All cats, of course, are beloved by Freya, whose chariot is pulled by cats.

> Bless my furred friend, O Vanadis,
> Bless the silent paws that pursue,
> Bless the quick teeth that hunt,
> Bless the sweet purr at the end of the day,
> Bless thou the finest cat in the world.

Freya Incense

Raven Kaldera

1 part wild strawberry leaves
1 part lavender
1 part basil
1 part rose petals
½ part runner bean blossoms
5 drops Lily of the Valley essential oil
¼ part Powdered Amber

(If you can't get it already powdered, take a small piece of low-grade amber and take sandpaper to it until you've worn away a small pile of it. Make sure that it is wholly amber and not copal or amber chips in plastic resin, as often happens today.)

Freya Prayer Beads
Raven Kaldera

Freya's stone is amber, so be sure to use real amber when you put these beads together. There's a lot of fake amber out there which is actually made of plastics. The beads that I used are suggestions; find what you can that is similarly-colored.

- ଓ *(Large amber bead)* Hail Freya, Vanadis, Lady who brings joy to the heart. May I walk in beauty wherever I go.
- ଓ *(Pale green aventurine bead)* Hail to the Spring Maiden! Teach me to start again with each new year.
- ଓ *(Striped white stone bead)* Beorc Beorc Beorc
- ଓ *(Gold metal bead)* Love always, magic everywhere, and joy.
- ଓ *(Pink glass/stone bead)* Hail to the Goddess of Love! Teach my heart to open to your most precious gift.
- ଓ *(Rose quartz bead)* Gyfu Gyfu Gyfu
- ଓ *(Gold metal bead)* Love always, magic everywhere, and joy.
- ଓ *(Golden-colored bead)* Hail to the Light-Bringer! Light my road when I fall into darkness.
- ଓ *(Clear quartz bead)* Wunjo Wunjo Wunjo Wunjo
- ଓ *(Gold metal bead)* Love always, magic everywhere, and joy.
- ଓ *(Glittering glass bead)* Hail to Brisingamen's Mistress! Teach me to always know my own worth.
- ଓ *(Deep green aventurine bead)* Feoh Feoh Feoh
- ଓ *(Gold metal bead)* Love always, magic everywhere, and joy.
- ଓ *(Large amber bead)* Hail Freya, Vanadis, Lady who brings joy to the heart. May I walk in beauty wherever I go.
- ଓ *(Red glass bead)* Hail to the Warrior Woman! Give me courage to fight again tomorrow.
- ଓ *(Yellow glass bead)* Sigil Sigil Sigil

- ❧ *(Gold metal bead)* Love always, magic everywhere, and joy.

- ❧ *(Purple amethyst bead)* Hail to the Mistress of Seidhr! Teach me the mysteries hidden behind the veil.

- ❧ *(Purple glass bead)* Peorth Peorth Peorth

- ❧ *(Gold metal bead)* Love always, magic everywhere, and joy.

- ❧ *(Green glass bead)* Hail to the Frith-Maker, Ambassador to Asgard! Teach me how to make peace among enemies.

- ❧ *(Pale orange carnelian bead)* Mannaz Mannaz Mannaz

- ❧ *(Gold metal bead)* Love always, magic everywhere, and joy.

- ❧ *(Blue glass bead)* Hail to the Widow who searched the worlds for her lost love! Help me to find happiness again after each loss.

- ❧ *(White pearl glass bead)* Chalc Chalc Chalc

- ❧ *(Gold metal bead)* Love always, magic everywhere, and joy.

- ❧ *(Large amber bead)* Hail Freya, Vanadis, Lady who brings joy to the heart. May I walk in beauty wherever I go.

Freya Bath Salts

Galina Krasskova

One of the things that I learned early on in my worship of Freya was that it's OK to celebrate our physicality, to rejoice in the blessings of incarnation—which can be annoying, inconvenient, and messy, but rich in blessings as well. Sometimes that's best done in small, seemingly insignificant ways. It adds up, after all. I first came to truly worship Freya through interacting with others who had a deep devotion to Her. In fact, one of the first offerings I ever made to Freya involved creating the following bath salts (from my own recipe) and sending them to a devotee of Freya for ritual use. While not the first interactions that I'd had with this Goddess, it was the first time that I called on Her, prayed to Her, poured out offerings (of Goldschlager liquor, for those interested) and felt any sort of connection to Her mysteries. I wanted to create something nice for my friend (and I knew she loved pampering herself with bath salts and whatnot) and asked for Freya's blessings. For those who might be interested, here is the recipe that I used. The "measurements" are approximate. Feel free to adapt to your own taste.

Base:

> 1 cup of Epsom salt
> 1/2 cup of kosher salt or (preferably) pink Himalayan salt
> ½ cup of baking soda
> ¼ cup of sweet almond oil *(for the skin, to keep the salts from being too harsh)*

To this base add the following:

> 4 parts damiana
> 2 parts rue
> 1 part raspberry leaf
> ½ part mint *(I like to use chocolate mint)*
> 1 part rose petals *(optional)*
> 1 part honey powder

15 drops Jasmine oil

1 or 2 tablespoons ground coffee *(It's really good for the skin, believe it or not.)*

10 drops lily of the valley or honeysuckle oil *(I believe I used honeysuckle oil for the first batch, and lily of the valley for the second. Try them both for yourself and decide what you like best.)*

2 tablespoons ground amber *(I took large pieces of amber, hammered them down into smaller chunks, put it in a mortar and pestle and ground it down to powder. It took a while.)*

Mix it all up thoroughly. You can grind it up if you want a finger grain to the salts. If I were doing these again, I'd probably add two tablespoons of gold glitter. (I've seen bath bombs that incorporated glitter and it's kind of cool. It adorns the skin long after the bath and that adornment, that sense of valuing oneself and one's embodiment, that simple celebration of beauty and physicality is something I associate with Freya's lessons)

I sent this to my friend with incense that I also associated with Freya (sadly, I've been unable to find that recipe) and a red candle. I told her to use the salts as a cleansing bath: prepare a bath, make an offering to Freya of the incense and whatever else she wanted to offer, light the candle and soak in the tub. Afterwards, she was to adorn herself in clothing and jewelry that made her feel beautiful. One of Freya's lessons is about valuing oneself, knowing one's personal work, and recognizing one's personal power, beauty, and holiness. Anything that helps the average woman do that, in my opinion, is a good and holy thing.

Hail Freya!

Prayers To Freya

Galina Krasskova

Someone asked me recently in an interview what I did first upon awakening. I said flippantly that I usually groan and wonder why I am awake, but then I stopped and gave the question the answer it actually deserved: I pray. My Odin shrine (one of them) is right at the foot of my bed (ironically right next to a Freya shrine) and it is usually the first thing that I see when I open my eyes. So when I wake up, I see the sacred images of a God I love more than breath itself, a God who has honed and blessed me in so many ways. My first thought upon really awakening, once the fog of sleep and desire for more sleep has been cleared away, is a prayer. I'm not talking about anything formal or structured, but simply "Gracious God, thank you." Or "Odin, be with me today," or sometimes – more often than not, actually – just a wordless outpouring of emotion. My thoughts turn to Him.

Still, I like morning rites and prayers, even though I rarely do anything quite so formalized. Mornings tend to be the only quiet time in my house, the time when I am alone and have the solitude to concentrate and prepare for my day. It's the time when I can ready myself to meet the world – whatever that may entail in the day that follows. I like the idea of having some way of centering that day around the Gods and ancestors, some way of reminding oneself that we're not alone as we scurry forth and bustle about.

Last year I was running a "Deity of the Month" on my blog and eventually I wrote about Freya. She is a magnificent Goddess, but not a Deity to Whom I had much personal devotion. I was delighted therefore when my friend Kira offered me the following morning prayer and with her permission, I share it here now.

A Morning Prayer for Freya

Kira R.

(Light a candle.)

Freya, Goddess of gold,
inspire me today.
Teach me to walk through my day
with pride in my own being,
with confidence,
with power.
Goddess of fiery passion,
bless me with the insight
to the marrow of my bones
that I am a person of worth
in the eyes of the Gods
the eyes of the ancestors
and of myself.
May I radiate this
and transforms all I meet.
That is my prayer for this day,
oh great and powerful Goddess,
that I may mirror Your presence throughout my day.
In return, I shall praise You always,
and lay amber before Your image,
consigning it to the sacred fires that burn
when the day is at its longest.
Hail Freya, shining Goddess of gold.
I praise You.

(Blow the candle out.)

Prayer To Freya

Galina Krasskova

Hail to the Lady of amber.
Hail to the Lady of steel.
Hail to the Lady of passion,
Bringer of luck,
Bestower of wealth.
You are the envy of all the Gods,
the treasure of the nine sacred worlds.

Freya, mighty and magnificent,
We praise Your name this day.
Ignite within us an awareness
of our own creative fire.
Ignite within us a passion,
to burn through the pale shadows of our lives
and find integrity and authenticity:
in all we do, in all we dream, in all we are.
Bless us, Freya, Lady of the Vanir,
and we shall hail You,
always.

Travels With Freya: How to Build a Portable Shrine for the Wandering Goddess

by Rebecca Buchanan

Portable shrines are a great and convenient way for modern Pagans to honor the Gods even while on the go. They are also easy to make: all you need are a few items which remind you of the God or Goddess for whom you are making the shrine, glue, and imagination. Below is my personal recipe for a Freya portable shrine; alter it as you see fit to create your own, unique shrine in honor of the Falcon Goddess (or any other Deity of your choice).

Items:

- ☙ One gift card box. Sturdy cardboard boxes with magnetic latches, such as those sold by Barnes and Noble, work best. Metallic gift card boxes, which can often be found at craft stores, also work but may prove problematic when passing through airport security. If you want to create a larger portable shrine, try a stationary gift box or even a fancy book gift box.

- ☙ One image of Freya, either your own or copied out of a book. Choose an image which has great meaning for you: a favorite from a childhood book on mythology, the photo of a statue you took at a museum, your own illustration done by your own hand, and so forth. I used the *IV Power: Freya* card from Kris Waldherr's *Goddess Tarot*.

- ☙ Jewelry charms, each of which in some way references a myth featuring Freya or an aspect of her personality: falcon feather and claw, boar and cat (domestic or wild), a golden chain, chariot, amber-colored beads or (if possible) real amber, and so on. Depending on your personal tastes, you may or may not be able to include a real (or synthetic) falcon feather, cat's claw, boar bristle, and so forth.

- ☙ Paint: blue or bluish–green (for her connection to the sea), and red or reddish–orange (for her association with amber, gold, and the falcon).

- ☙ Fine gold dust, shimmer sand, or golden sprinkles.

ও Brush and bowl of water.

ও Superglue.

ও Three stones or pieces of sea glass, flat enough to be stacked.

Building the Shrine

I opted for a small gift card box with a magnetic latch. I poured out some of the red paint into a plastic plate and thoroughly mixed in some of the gold dust. I then painted the exterior of the box with the mixture. Once that was dry, I opened the box and painted the interior bluish–green.

Next, I stacked and glued the three stones on the inside, bottom of the box, creating a miniature, primitive altar. I made sure to hold the stones in place until the glue hardened. (Since the stones are the heaviest items, stacking them on the bottom helps to balance the shrine.) I then glued the Freya image to the inside cover of the box. (If you feel so inclined, augment the image with gold dust, markers, paint, gold thread, or anything else that strikes your fancy.)

After arranging and rearranging the jewelry charms (making sure the box would still close securely), I glued them in place. Give the glue time to dry before you set the shrine upright.

Finally, I cut several strands of golden thread, making sure they were long enough to wrap around the box. I braided and knotted the thread, smeared some glue along the spine of the box, and held the braid in place until it was secure. I then loosely tied the ends of the braid in a bow. (The magnetic latch makes the ribbon unnecessary, but it is a pretty decorative touch.)

That's it! The portable shrine is small enough to tuck inside my carry–on bag, where I can both keep an eye on it and keep it handy; I would hate to lose it if an airport inspector considered it contraband or my luggage was misplaced. When I am at home, the portable shrine sits on my bookshelf beside my books on Heathenry and Norse mythology.

Hopefully my own recipe has given you a few ideas for creating a portable shrine of your own. Now get to it!

Invocation to Freya

Beatriz Prat

We call upon the Great Goddess of the Vanir
Who is also known as Vanadis.
Freya, Shamanic mistress of Magick and the art of Seidr,
Teach us as you taught the All-father Odin.
You who fly through the night with your falcon-feathered Cloak
And who rides your chariot driven by cats and her boar Hildisvini,
Shapeshift our lives to embrace your mysteries.
We invoke your powers as warrior
To help protect our hearth and home.
Grant us prosperity and riches,
Surround us with gold and jewels.
You who wear the necklace known as Brisingamen,
Gifted by pleasure,
You who are wanted by Giants and men
For the power of sexuality and fertility,
Grant us beauty and love.
Show us how to honor our bodies as we honor yours.
Embraces us as you would,
For we are your daughters.
We praise you, we worship you,
And we welcome you into our lives.
Grant us your presence! Hail Freya!

Poetry

For The Vanadis

Gudrun of Mimirsbrunnr

Hail to the Spring Maiden
on the Equinox morning
as she rises and walks the fields;
flowers bloom in her footsteps
and the earth wakes anew.
O Freya snowdrop-bedecked,
wake my life anew and teach me wonder,
for I am dull and grey with years of burdens
and I have forgotten the mystery of the rising seed.

Hail to the Laughing Dancer
on Beltane morning
as she weaves the maypole's ribbons
and the wombs of women are filled
as they lie with their loves on the turned earth.
O Freya bright in green and gold
fill me with life like the pealing waterfall,
for I am dull and dry with years of thirsting
and I have forgotten the mystery of the branching trees.

Hail to the Summer Queen
on the solstice morning
as she turns the head to love
and the body to loving,
and opens hearts with a touch.
O Freya with tongue and thighs of honey,
open me up like a ripe fruit
for I am dull and withered with years of hunger
and I have forgotten the mystery of the tender blossom.

Hail to the Jeweled Lady
on Lammas morning
whose flesh is her treasure,

and worth all the greatest treasure,
all that gold can buy.
O Freya Brisingamen-Bearer,
help me to know my own worth
for I am dull and shrunken with years of downcast eyes
and I have forgotten the mystery of the proud glance.

Hail to the Warrior Woman
on the equinox morning,
white-armored, choosing the slain
by her own glorious criteria,
harbor to the defenders of beauty.
O Freya who rides with Valkyries,
give me strength to defend all that I love
for I am dull and frightened with years of defeat
and I have forgotten the mystery of shieldmates in love.

Hail to the Mistress of Seid
on Hallows' morning,
mysterious and seductive through the gauze
of her own wisdom, glowing confident
in the ways of women's magic.
O Freya wreathed in veils of smoke,
open my eyes to possibility
for I am dull and blind with years of illusion
and I have forgotten the mystery of the candle's flame.

Hail to the ambassador to Asgard
on the solstice morning
a ray of light in a cold white world,
bringing the green of Vanaheim's fields
and the gold of Vanaheim's courage.
Hail Freya Frithmaker, Bridge-Builder,
help me to hold out my hands with a smile
for I am dull and closed-in with years of mistrust

and I have forgotten the mystery of the open arms.

Hail to Odr's widow
on Imbolc morning
searching for her lost husband,
whipped by salt-sea wind,
waiting in the winter harbor for her father's return.
O Freya weeping tears of amber
help me to wake to the dawn of rebirth
for I am dull and beaten with years of mourning
and I have forgotten the mystery of the melting frost.

O Vanadis, may I be open to all you have to teach
in spite of all I have become
and because of all I yet could be.

In Praise Of The Vanadis

Gudrun of Mimirsbrunnr

Behind the Door of Gold lies the darkness of the Gap,
The knocker is a sunbeam and on the Door I tap,
It opens to the Stone of Power where my Lady has her Way,
Where fields of darkness yield to light as sunrise paints the day.

The Maiden of the Spring who brings the start of every year
Has bought my soul's shy maidenhead with tenderness and tears.
The Lover of the Summer who comes in finest gold
Has bought my soul's green maidenhead with truer stories told.

The Warrior of the Autumn, amidst souls like fallen leaves,
Has bought my soul's bright maidenhead with courage like sweet
mead,
But the Witch of Winter's Fire, shining golden on the hearth,
Has taken me beneath her veil to learn her darkest arts.

Behind the Door of Gold lies the Mystery of the Road,
And I would travel down to pluck the seeds that she has sowed,
I weave and wear the woman's arts as the Vanadis foretold,
And her song rings through my body as her gold burns in my soul.

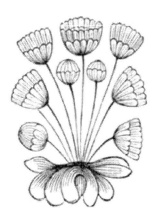

In Praise Of The Vanadis

Gudrun of Mimirsbrunnr

1. Be-hind the Door of Gold lies the dark-ness of the Gap, The knock-er is a sun-beam and on the door I tap, it o-pens to the Stone of Power where my La-dy has her way, Where fields of dark-ness yield to light as sun-rise paints the day. 2. The Maid-en of the Spring who brings the start of ev-ery year Has bought my soul's shy maid-en-head with ten-der-ness and tears, The Lov-er of the Sum-mer who comes in fi-nest gold Has

bought my soul 'green mai-den-head with tru-er sto-ries told. 3. The

war-rior of the au-tumn, 'midst souls like fal-len leaves, Has

bought my soul's bright mai-den-head with cou-rage like sweet

mead. But the Witch of Win-ter's Fi-re, shi-ning gol-den on the

hearth Has ta-ken me be-neath her veil to

learn her dark-est arts. 4. Be-hind the Door of

Gold lies the mys-tery of the Road, And I would tra-vel

down to pluck the seeds that she has sowed, I

weave and wear the wo - man's arts as the Van - a - dis fore-

told And her song rings through my bo - dy as her

gold burns in my soul.

Tears in the Ocean

Michaela Macha

I hardly noticed when he was going,
I didn't think to say him goodbye.
I missed my chance on that day, little knowing
He would not return and I'd never know why.

I hid at my home, hid my sorrow and rage,
I buried my grieving ever so deep;
But love freed my feelings and feet from their cage:
I set out to search him, and started to weep.

Chorus:
My tears in the ocean turned amber and gold,
My tears at the Tree were filling the Well;
My tears in the field made the flowers unfold,
My tears at the river were flowing to Hel.

I wandered the wastelands, I searched far and near,
As falcon I flew over mountains and hill,
From daybreak to nightfall and year after year,
And in all my dreams I am searching him still.

Chorus:
My tears in the ocean...

I roamed through the realms of the quick and the dead,
I searched on the other side of the sky;
No place in Nine Worlds where I did not tread,
And wheresoever I went, I did cry.

Chorus:
My tears in the winter turned crystals of ice,
My tears in the night, seven stars for the sea.

My tears fell as diamonds, a find for the wise;
My tears they brought comfort to any but me.

In Midgard I talked to the daughters of men,
To widows and orphans and all who have lost;
In memories, their loved ones were living again,
Their songs were burning like fires in frost.

Chorus:
The wyrd of all worlds and all wights is to perish,
I wept for the fate of each man and each god.
I wept for all we hold dear and we cherish,
But most of all, I wept for my Od.

I forget how he smelled, I forget how he smiled,
But I shall always remember our love.
I seek for his charm in the eyes of our child,
And I hear his voice in the sound of her laugh.

Chorus:
My tears in the ocean...

Tears in the Ocean

Michaela Macha

I hardly noticed when he was going, I didn't think to say him good-bye. I missed my chance on that day little knowing he would not return and I'd never know why. I hid at my home, hid my sorrow and rage, I buried my grieving ever so deep, But love freed my feelings and feet from their cage, I set out to search him and started to weep. My tears in the ocean turned amber and gold, __ my tears at the Tree were filling the Well. My tears in the field made the flowers unfold, __ my tears at the river were flowing to Hel. I wandered the wastelands, I searched far and near, as falcon I flew over mountains and hills, From daybreak to nightfall and year after year, and in all my dreams I am searching him still. My tears in the ocean turned amber and gold, __ my tears at the Tree were filling the Well. My tears in the field made the flowers unfold, __ my tears at the river were flowing to Hel. I

roamed through the realms of the quick and the dead, I

searched on the oth - - er side of the sky, No

place in Nine Worlds__where I did not tread, and where-so-ev-er I

went, I did cry. My tears in the win-ter turned cry-stals and ice,__ my

tears in the night, sev-en stars for the sea. My

tears fell as dia-monds, a find for the wise,__ my

tears they brought com-fort to a-ny but me. In

Mid-gard I talked to the daugh-ters of men, to

wid-ows and or-phans and all who have lost, In

mem-ories their loved ones were liv-ing a-gain, their

songs were bur-ning like fires__ and frost. The

wyrd of all worlds and all wights is to per-ish, I

wept for the fate of each man and each god.

I wept for all we hold dear and we cher-ish, but most of all, I

wept for my Od. I for--get how he smelled, I for-

get how he smiled, but I shall al-ways re-mem-ber our love, I

seek for his charm in the eyes of our child, and I hear his voice in the

sound of her laugh. My tears in the o-cean turned am-ber and gold, __ my

tears at the Tree were fill-ing the Well. My tears in the field made the

flow-ers un-fold, __ my tears at the riv-er were flow-ing to Hel. My

tears in the o-cean turned am-ber and gold, __ my tears at the Tree were

fill-ing the Well. My tears in the field made the flow-ers un-fold, __ my

tears at the riv-er were flow-ing to Hel.

(Od) Freya's Search

Michaela Macha

Each day at first I thought he would return yet;
Each nightfall found me waiting still, and cold.
And when I wept, face turned toward the sunset,
Some thought they saw me crying tears of gold.

In empty hours filled by fruitless yearning
The questions "why" and "where" pierce like a dart.
Nine realms I searched till soul and feet were burning,
The only place I found him was my heart.

To know my love he was nor first nor last one,
But of all lovers, only husband he.
With only memories of him to grasp on,
Immortal years seem stretching long to me.

They shake their heads and tell me to forget him,
That life goes on, and all its pleasures too.
But I shall never cease to mourn and miss him,
Because he was the one I loved most true.

Hymn to Freyja I

Rebecca Buchanan

Sea-Bright daughter of Njord
Flaxen-haired wife of Odr
 forever mourning
 lashes glittering
  with gold-rich tears
 wandering mountains
  steep shores
  dark bogs
  wide meadows
 ever searching
 ever seeking
Weeping Lady
 tears the hidden treasure of the world

Hymn to Freyja II

Rebecca Buchanan

Sea-Bright Goddess
Flaxen hair braided with gold
 amber
 falcon feathers
Mistress of the Honored Dead
Who chooses heroes
 to feast in her many-seated hall
Who rides into battle
 on the broad back of Hildisvani
  gold-bristled boar
Who parades in glory in her chariot
 drawn by great-eared lynxes
Freyja
Great Lady

Hymn to Freyja III
Rebecca Buchanan

Amber Lady
Bearer of Brisingamen
     forged with love and skill
Bearer of Valshamr
     cloak of stealth and transformation
Mistress of the Valkyries
     chooser of the noble dead
Bountiful Giver
Great Sow
Honored in many lands
     by many names
But known by all
     as Goddess Most Fair

Freyja Haiku I
Rebecca Buchanan

mistress falcon, she
soars, ever
searching the nine worlds

Freyja Haiku II
Rebecca Buchanan

she wanders the shore,
weeping, her
tears our bright treasure

Freya's Return

Joseph Kenyon

And then there were circumstances
growing all together:
some seemed to be solid items
others milky, unsure.

These are the mists, darling,
mists of a goddess
who gathers around all endings,
all emergences.

She'll run up your coast
if she be let,
plundering your shores,
carrying off your old hoard
into her own carved worlds.

Don't give into the dizzying sense
of falling into steepness.
Don't step away from your body
or hold your breath.
Instead, feel the thought-dead deity
beginning to rise,

feel her crawl up your esophagus
and out your mouth,
slithering down your belly
onto the porcelain,

smiling into the fertile darkness,
not knowing, not caring
where you are supposed to be going,
but only who is calling you
by a very old name.

Upon Inviting In Freya

Jim Johnston

Words cannot speak of what we shared,
the dooms and the Norns were unprepared,
within your breast your heart-beat veered,
within your eyes I glimpsed the Wyrd.

Star after star shone down and through us,
hue after hue gave colour to us,
light after light found light within us,
look after look lodged gnosis in us.

Knowledge and lore and finding runes,
movement and light-play and binding tunes,
cloak after cloak was shed and abandoned,
knot after knot was opened and bound.

Three after three gave rise to the four,
breath after breath found us wanting more,
soul upon soul gave us wings to soar,
the wind in your grasp was a whispering roar.

Freya and Hel looked out from your eyes,
the Bifrost Bridge scaled infinite skies,
your fingers bound me with wonderful ties
to a moment of moments, an inner sunrise.

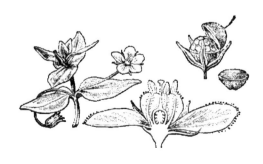

Praise Be To The Goddess

Erin Lale

In olden times all knew your name,
And adoration followed fame,
A million lips of many lands
Once sang and worshipped you and danced
In secret grove and temple white,
At noon and even and by starlight,
On frozen tor and bitter plain,
And steaming island in the rain,
On sea-ship proud and sloping farm,
Your children all you kept from harm,
In gentle town, on mountain steep,
What they planted so they reaped,
Your witches knew no evil spell,
And none yet feared the name of Hel.
Oh Goddess-Mother Freya true!
A thousand years your lips were few,
But now your childrens' souls recall
The joys of earth and holy hall.
We dance again by midnight sea
When seasons turn and hearts are free,
Abandon fear, abandon doom,
For mirth and pleasure now make room,
We laugh and cry both women and men,
We eat your grain and praise with pen,
We try to heal the hurts of earth
Which as your body gave us birth.
Oh Goddess-Woman Freya free!
You've given back my soul to me.

Lady of Fólkvangr

Rebecca L. Brown

Lady of Fólkvangr,
to you comes your share of battle-weary warriors
to dwell within your halls.
What men and women feast there at your tables?
What men and women do you gather to Sessrúmnir
to fill your many seats?
Around your tables the brave, the fearless and the noble.
And in those many seats the valiant and heroic dead.
The wish of many a warrior is that in death
His honoured ancestors will welcome him to your side.

Freya's Kriger

Jeff Davis

I was once a soldier on the field.
Fought for a cause greater than myself, or so I thought.
My strength exhausted, I did not yield.
Time run out, I breathed my last.

Opened my eyes to see a fair and fierce lady warrior.
Am I dreaming? Where am I now?
No! I was not finished, or so I thought.
Come with me valiant warrior; your time here is done.

In an instance the field is but memory.
What is this place of ethereal beauty?
Why does it seem somehow familiar?
As I walk, I see a Lady of uncommon beauty in the distance.

I see Her smile the closer I get.
Her radiance so bright I can no longer look direct.
A deep sense of respect and love rise within.
To one knee I go because my heart compels me.

With head bowed and eyes closed.
I feel Her radiate pure light and love.
Content to remain, She touches my shoulder.
A rush of energy goes through me to penetrate my heart.

In that moment all pain rises to the surface
And is gone in an instant.
All warrior's reserve lost, tears flood
And I can no longer hold the pain.
You have fought well. Rest awhile.
Yes, my Lady.

When the time is right, you will return to Midgard.
The battles will be different from the past.
My mind races, my emotions are tumult, my will falters.
She senses all these things within me
And smiles with reassuring confidence.

You will face many things but do not lose heart.
Your disir will watch over you, she will be your guide.
I will always be with you, even when you forget.
How could I ever forget you my Lady?

You have much to learn young warrior.
Yes, my Lady, you are far wiser than me.
You will remember Me and this place when the time is right.
All manner of questions run through my being but I dare not ask.

The truth is I am more than content
To be in Her presence and feel Her light.
To hear Her words no matter the subject.
My time in this place will be short, shorter than I like, I can feel it.
She has a mission for me, yet I am reluctant to leave.

It is time to return.
Take courage while in Midgard.
You are chosen by Me. I will love and guard you.
Why me, why now? Questions matter not.

Bright flash of light and Asgard is gone from sight.
Where am I now? This place, all too familiar.
I am on earth. Why am I here?
Why do I have this nagging question?
Why do I feel like an old warrior? Maybe I am.
Maybe someday I will understand.

In the Mists

Erik

(Dedicated to Freya.)

My love lies in the Mists,
Hidden and alone.
Shrouded from sight,
So far away.

I know she is out there,
Though I can see her not.
Through endless bank of fog,
She waits.

What is she waiting for?
Why does she not come forth?
In the Mists she walks,
So far away.

I cannot see her,
Though I know she is there.
She is shrouded from sight,
But not from my heart.
I cannot see her,
But I can feel her.

In the Mists she waits,
So far away.
I must find her,
Before the Beast.

In the Mists lurks something else,
A Beast.
It hunts for her,

Nose to the wind.
It closes in on her,
And will carry her away from me
Forever.

I must find her,
Before the Beast.
She is out in the Mists,
And I must save her.

I must find her,
She will protect me,
And I will protect her,
And the Beast will find neither of us.

My love waits in the Mists,
Seeking me, as I search for her.
Should I try and go to her,
Reach out, seek, to find?
Or wait for her here,
That she may find me?

If I seek her out,
Will I be gone when she would find me?
If I do not go in search of her,
Will she never come to me?
Do I delve into the Mists,
Seeking my shrouded love,
And risk losing myself?

Is she drawn to me,
As I am to her,
Though we know each other not?
We are one,
Temporarily cleft in twain.

The Mist rises before me,
Cruelly hiding my love from my eyes,
Though not from my heart.
I cannot see her,
But I can feel her,
And I know she waits for me.

Into the Mists I shall go,
Blind though unafraid,
Seeking her to whom I belong,
And she who belongs to me.
I seek,
I search,
One day to find,
My truest, deepest love,
In the Mists.

In each other's arms at last,
We ascend to Sessrumnir,
Having earned Freya's gift.
No longer lost,
No longer seeking,
Safe at last,
No longer,
In the Mists.

Freya's Rose
Michael Schütz

Freya's fragrance fills the air,
Embracing you so playfully-
Freya's rose of fiery red.

The rose's chalice now invites you,
Nectar-moist from last night's dream-
Freya's rose of fiery red.

Cool like velvet are the leaves,
Fanning embers to a fire-
Freya's rose of fiery red.

Like red lips the petals beckon,
Opening up invitingly-
Freya's rose of fiery red.

Freya's Cup of Passion
Michael Schütz

From Freya's hand you receive the cup of passion.
Once your lips have touched the rim, her fire sets you in flames.
Sweetly the drop flows down the throat, and you've fallen to her.
Freya's favor carries you off
As the flow in your mouth runs through you.
Climbing highest peaks of lust, you plunge into sorrow's valley;
Give Freya yourself with body and soul,
Even though the last sip is bitter.

𝔄 Sacrifice 𝔗o Freya

Michael Schütz

What can I sacrifice to you, Freya?
The taste of sweet honey that melts on the tongue?
Whatever you give, give it with a full heart.

What can I give to you, Graceful One?
Do you desire a blossom's beauty that unfolds the heart?
Whatever you give, give it your way.

What can I sacrifice, Free One?
Do you wish the ethereal smell
Of a perfume that arouses the senses?
Whatever it is, put your emotions into it.

What can I offer you, Muse?
Do you long for a song that fills the soul with joy?
Whatever you give, small or great, it's part of you that you give.

It is a moment full of passion you dedicate Freya,
whether from the depths of tears
or on the crests of joy,
it will be Freya's.

Catching Freya

Michael Schütz

Try to bind her, and she'll storm away,
a free falcon circling the sky.
Invite her in, and she'll return to you,
From her journey, time and again.

Seek to close her in behind bars,
You'll just find that you've caught yourself;
Without feeling, hard grows your heart;
sensuousness flies in falcon garb.

Try to catch her and empty's your hand,
Let her go, and she will consume you;
Fully embrace her, she'll open you up
and give you all the fullness of life.

Freya the free one, the strong one, the wild,
Giving gifts with generous hand;
From this fullness love may prosper,
Like herself, so unbound and free.

About the Editor

Gefion Vanirdottir lives in Kitchener, Ontario, Canada with her parents, a dog, and a bearded dragon. This is her first published work.

You can find her word-trove online at:

https://adventuresinvanaheim.wordpress.com/